To dear Liz,
Wishing you a very happy
21st birthday,
"And lots of cooking!!",
Love Robyn & Selwyn.
1973.

Best of the Bake-Off Recipes

Best of the Bake-Off Recipes

Selected and compiled by Trevor Wilson

From the finalists and prizewinners
of over one hundred thousand recipes submitted
to all the Butter-White Wings Bake-Offs.

URE SMITH • SYDNEY • LONDON

First published in Australia in 1969 by
Ure Smith Pty Ltd, 155 Miller Street
North Sydney, NSW, 2060
London Office: Horwitz Group Books
88 Farringdon Street, EC4

National Library of Australia Registry Number Aus 69-2457
Library of Congress Catalog Card Number 70-92565
Printed in Hong Kong by Lee Fung Printing Company

Contents

Desserts

Pastries and Breads

Biscuits

Illustrations

Some of the International Judges of the Butter-White Wings Bake-Offs

Graham Kerr, noted gourmet, author, TV personality and Chairman of the Bake-Off with Monica Sheridan, TV personality in Dublin and UK, authoress of cookbooks, and noted cooking authority of Dublin TV

Edoardo Moglia, General Manager, Hotel Real Fini, Modena, Italy. International Bake-Off Judge 1968

Napua Stevens of the Ilikai Hotel, Hawaii, and Lucien Chassignat of the Hotel Meurice, Paris. Tw of the international judges at the 1967 Bake-Off

Monica Sheridan, Edoardo Moglia and Graham Kerr during the judging of the Grand Champion of the 1968 Bake-Off

Sr. Antonio Prantera of the Helio Cabala, Roma. One of the three international judges at the 1967 Bake-Off

The chef from the Southern Cross Hotel cooking a main dish during a Bake-Off

Guest of Honour Lady Angus, herself a Cordon Bleu Cook, with Grand Champion 1, Mrs Berwyn McQuitty of Burnie, Tasmania

There is nothing like a contest to bring out the best. That is why this is a great cook book. It has not had one author, it has had hundreds—selected from thousands. To qualify for inclusion you would have entered your finest recipe in the Butter-White Wings Bake-Off. In the unlikely event that it survived the critical examination of the preliminary judges and the stiff competition, it would have reached the state finals and thus qualified for the national finals. It would have been appraised by experts, cooked by experts, tasted by experts. The Grand Champions are chosen by some of the world's finest judges of good food. It is a rare privilege to have the opportunity to compile such a book of finalists and prizewinners from countless thousands of recipes.

Some of these recipes are elaborate. Most are simple. All have been tested in Australia's most important and exciting cookery contest—truly a prize-winning cookery book. But perhaps the most important achievement of these recipes is not that they have won prizes but that they have been tested and tested again. Although they have been tested by judges of international reputation from Australia, from France, Ireland, Italy and other countries throughout the world, they are not the sophisticated creations of an Escoffier. They owe their origins to those most discerning judges—housewives from all over the country.

The Australian Dairy Produce Board and White Wings Limited are proud of their Bake-Off and they have reason to be. It has become a national institution and this collection is tangible proof of the great and growing interest in good food and good cooking in Australia and throughout the world.

Cheese Chicken Surprises

2 cups plain flour
pinch salt
pinch cayenne pepper
4 oz. butter
3 oz. cream cheese
1 egg-yolk
squeeze lemon juice
approximately 1 tablespoon water
milk to glaze

FILLING
4 oz. bacon, chopped
1 onion, chopped
½ cup milk
1 dessertspoon butter
2 eggs
1 cup cooked, diced chicken
1 cup grated cheddar cheese
¼ teaspoon celery salt
pinch pepper
1 dessertspoon finely chopped parsley

Sift flour, salt, cayenne into bowl. Rub butter and cream cheese into flour until mixture resembles fine breadcrumbs. Mix egg-yolk, lemon juice and water and add to flour mixture to form a firm dough. Chill. Roll out on lightly floured board to ⅛-in. thickness and cut into 3-in. rounds. Line small buttered patty pans with pastry. Cut same number of rounds, using 2-in. cutter for tops. Half fill each patty tin with chicken mixture, moisten edges with milk, cover with tops and press edges together. With sharp knife, make slit in top of each pie, glaze with milk and bake in hot oven, 10 to 15 minutes or until golden brown.

FILLING: Lightly fry bacon in small saucepan, add onion to milk and cook over medium heat for a few minutes. Add butter and cool. Beat eggs lightly and add all ingredients, blend well together.

Cheese Tricorns

1½ cups plain flour
¼ teaspoon salt
pinch cayenne pepper
4 oz. butter
6 oz. grated cheddar cheese
2 egg-yolks
1 teaspoon lemon juice
1 cup finely chopped cucumber
1 cup finely chopped watercress, or shallots
1 6½-oz. can crabmeat
mayonnaise

Sift flour, salt and cayenne pepper together. Rub in butter. Add cheese. Beat together egg-yolks and lemon juice. Mix with dry ingredients to make a stiff dough (add a little water if necessary). Turn on to floured board. Roll out thinly about ⅛ in. Cut into 4-in. rounds. Prick each round with a fork. Cut quilted foil into 4-in. rounds. Place 1 round of pastry on each piece of foil and press gently. Form triangular shells by pinching foil together tightly at 3 equal intervals to form corners. Bake in moderate oven 10 minutes until a light straw colour. Cool. Fill tricorn with mixture of cucumber, watercress and crabmeat, moistened with mayonnaise.

Ham Savouries

4 oz. butter
¼ teaspoon salt
1 cup plain flour
¾ cup mashed potatoes
1 egg-white for glazing

FILLING
1 oz. butter
1 small onion, finely chopped
8 oz. chopped ham
2 tablespoons corn relish
1 tablespoon mustard sauce
½ teaspoon paprika
¼ teaspoon pepper

Add butter, salt and flour to cool mashed potatoes and work into a dough. Chill 30 minutes. Roll out to ¼-in. thickness. Using a scone cutter, cut into 2-in. circles and put 1 teaspoon of filling on each. Fold in half and pinch edges together, forming a pastie shape. Brush with lightly-beaten egg-white and bake on ungreased baking trays in moderately hot oven 15 minutes. Serve hot with salad vegetables.

FILLING: Melt butter and sauté onion until tender. Remove from heat and add ham, relish, mustard sauce, paprika and pepper.

Bacon and Sausage Plait
(See recipe on page 22)

Cheese Salmon Strudel

1½ cups plain flour
¼ teaspoon salt
1 teaspoon baking powder
4 oz. butter
¼ cup finely-grated cheese
cold water
milk for glazing

FILLING
1 tablespoon finely chopped onion
2 oz. butter
1 tablespoon plain flour
¼ cup evaporated milk
16 oz. can salmon, drained
¼ cup salmon liquid
salt and cayenne pepper to taste
grated lemon rind to flavour
1 egg, beaten
¼ cup chopped parsley

Sift flour, salt and baking powder together. Rub in butter and cheese and mix to a dough with water. Chill pastry while preparing filling. Knead pastry lightly and roll out on floured board to a rectangle. Arrange filling in centre. Glaze edges and roll up. Seal top and ends. Glaze with milk. Bake in hot oven for 10 minutes, reduce heat and bake further 30 minutes. Serve hot or cold.

FILLING: Heat butter, add onion and cook until tender, but not browned. Add flour and blend, add milk and salmon liquid and stir until it boils and thickens. Add pepper, salt, lemon rind, salmon, egg and parsley.

Spiced Cheese Appetisers

1½ cups self-raising flour
2 tablespoons cornflour
½ teaspoon salt
½ teaspoon dry mustard
2 tablespoons dried cream of chicken soup
4 oz. butter
4 oz. grated cheese
1 egg, slightly beaten
milk
2 oz. crushed toasted almonds
pinch cayenne

Sift flour, cornflour, salt, mustard, add dried soup. Rub in butter, add 3 oz. grated cheese and mix well. Make well in centre and add egg and a little milk if necessary to make a dough, knead lightly. Mix in almonds and roll out thinly on floured surface. Cut into fancy shapes, place on buttered biscuit trays, brush tops with milk and dust with remaining grated cheese and a sprinkling of cayenne. Bake in moderate oven 10 to 15 minutes..

Savoury Bacon Rolls

1 oz. compressed yeast
3 teaspoons sugar
1 teaspoon plain flour
½ pint milk
4 oz. butter
2 teaspoons salt
2 tablespoons sugar
3 cups flour
1 egg-yolk
1 slightly beaten egg to glaze

FILLING
3 large onions, chopped
1-2 oz. butter
8 oz. bacon, chopped very finely
1 teaspoon white pepper

Put yeast in small bowl with sugar. Stir with a spoon until yeast becomes liquid, sprinkle with 1 teaspoon flour and leave in a warm place. Combine milk, butter, salt and sugar in a saucepan and heat only until lukewarm, stirring occasionally. Sift flour twice into large mixing bowl, pour milk mixture and liquid yeast mixture into flour, add egg-yolk and stir with a wooden spoon. Beat dough about 3 minutes until it is smooth and no longer sticks to the hand, sprinkle a little flour on top, cover with a tea towel and leave in warm place until doubled in volume, about 1 to 1¼ hours. When doubled in volume, put it on a floured board, pull out edge of dough, put about 1 level teaspoon of filling on dough, fold edge over and cut out with a small glass to resemble a half moon. Repeat. Put rolls on a scone tray and leave to rise again, about 15 minutes. Glaze with slightly beaten egg and bake in very hot oven for 5 to 7 minutes or until a light brown colour. Slide on to a tea towel and while still hot rub over with a slice of bacon to give an extra shine. Bacon Rolls are best served hot, but can be reheated in quilted aluminium foil in a moderate oven for 10 to 15 minutes.

FILLING: Fry chopped onions in butter until golden brown. Cool. Mix bacon with onion, and add pepper. Combine well.

Cheese and Walnut Loaf

2 cups (8 oz.) self-raising flour
1 teaspoon dry mustard
1 teaspoon salt
pepper
4 oz. butter
4 oz. grated cheddar cheese
1 oz. chopped walnuts
2 eggs
5 oz. milk

Sift flour, mustard, salt and pepper together. Rub in butter until it resembles dry breadcrumbs. Add cheese and walnuts. Mix to a soft dropping consistency with beaten eggs and milk. Place in a greased loaf tin and bake 45 to 50 minutes in moderate oven (350°G, 375°E). When cold cut in slices and butter. Serve with cheese and salad.

Mushroom Turnovers

9 oz. cream cheese (at room temperature)
4 oz. butter (at room temperature)
12 oz. plain flour

MUSHROOM FILLING
3 tablespoons butter
1 large onion, finely chopped
½ lb. mushrooms, finely chopped
¼ teaspoon thyme
½ teaspoon salt
black pepper to taste
2 tablespoons flour
¼ cup sour cream

Mix the cheese and butter thoroughly. Add flour and work with fingers or pastry blender till smooth. Chill well for at least 30 minutes. Preheat oven to 450°. Roll dough to ⅛ in. thick on a lightly-floured surface and cut into rounds with 3-in. biscuit cutter. Place a teaspoonful of filling on each and fold over filling. Press edges together with a fork. Prick top crusts. Place on an ungreased sheet and bake till lightly brown, about 15 minutes.

FILLING: In a saucepan, heat butter, add onion, brown lightly. Add mushrooms and cook, stirring often, about 3 minutes. Add thyme, salt and pepper and sprinkle with flour. Stir in cream and cook gently till thick.

Cheese Prinskies

PASTRY
3 oz. butter
½ cup water
½ cup plain flour
2 eggs
⅓ cup coarsely grated cheddar cheese

SAUCE
2 oz. butter
¼ cup plain flour
1½ cups milk
½ cup coarsely grated cheese
½ teaspoon nutmeg
½ teaspoon paprika
¼ teaspoon salt
½ cup fine dry breadcrumbs
4 oz. butter

In a small saucepan over medium heat bring to a boil the butter and water. Add ½ cup flour all at once and stir vigorously until the mixture comes away from the sides of the pan and forms a ball. Put it in the small bowl of an electric mixer and add 2 eggs, one at a time, beating thoroughly at high speed after each addition. Fold in the grated cheddar cheese. Form the dough into two strips, each about 12 in. long and 2 in. wide. Bake the strips on a greased baking sheet in a moderately hot oven (375°) for 40 minutes. Let the strips cool on a rack. In a saucepan over medium heat melt 2 oz. butter, add ¼ cup flour and stir until smooth. Gradually add the milk and cook the sauce, stirring constantly, until it is thick. Add the cheese and continue cooking until the cheese melts. Remove the sauce from the heat and stir in the nutmeg, paprika and salt. Spread approximately ⅛ of the sauce on one pastry strip and invert the other strip over it. Press gently together, sticking with a little more sauce if necessary. Spread the top with a thin layer of sauce and coat it with fine breadcrumbs. Invert and repeat the process on the bottom. With a very sharp knife cut the strip crosswise into 12 strips. Spread ends and cut surfaces with remaining sauce and coat with breadcrumbs. Sauté the strips in butter in a heavy skillet over medium heat until golden brown on all sides, adding more butter if necessary. Serve immediately.

Cottage Cheese Rolls

(Makes 12)
2 cups self-raising flour
½ teaspoon salt
3 oz. butter
about ¼ pint milk
beaten egg or extra milk for glazing
poppy seeds or parmesan cheese

CHEESE FILLING
1 cup dry cottage cheese
1 tablespoon plain flour
1 teaspoon salt
1 egg
¼ cup chopped parsley

Sift flour and salt, add butter cut into small pieces. Rub until mixture resembles fine breadcrumbs. Add milk gradually and mix quickly with a fork to a soft dough. Turn on to a floured board and knead lightly until smooth. Roll out dough to ¼-in. thickness and cut with floured knife into tall triangles with 2½-in. base. Spoon 1 teaspoon of cheese filling on to wide end of each triangle. Roll up and seal ends with beaten egg and shape into crescents. Brush with egg and sprinkle with poppy seed or parmesan. Bake in hot oven 12 to 15 minutes until golden brown.

CHEESE FILLING: Mix cheese, flour, salt, egg and parsley in small bowl.

Cheese Crescents

8 oz. butter
2 eggs
½ cup milk
3½-4 cups self-raising flour
beaten egg to glaze

CHEESE FILLING
12 oz. cheese
2 eggs
pinch pepper

Cream butter until soft, add eggs, one at a time, mix well. Fold in sifted flour, a little at a time, alternately with milk, using hands to make a soft pliable dough. Knead a little, wrap in foil and chill 30 minutes. Divide pastry into portions the size of golf balls and roll into small circles, place a full teaspoon of Cheese Filling on each and fold over in the shape of a half moon. Put about ½ in. apart on buttered baking trays and brush with beaten egg. Bake in moderately hot oven about 20 minutes until puffed and golden brown. May be eaten warm or cold. Store in airtight tin.

CHEESE FILLING: Grate cheese coarsely. Add eggs, one at a time and mix well. Season with pepper.

Cheese Press Cookies

4 oz. butter
4 oz. shredded cheddar cheese
1 egg-yolk
pinch cayenne
¼ teaspoon salt
2 cups plain flour

Cream butter and cheese until light and smooth. Beat in egg-yolk. Sift flour, salt and cayenne and blend into mixture. Use a biscuit press to stamp out fancy shapes. Bake in moderate oven 10 to 12 minutes.

Crispy Cheese Rounds

1½ cups plain flour
pinch salt and pepper
3 oz. butter
2 tablespoons crushed corn cereal
1 egg-yolk
water to mix
beaten egg for glazing
extra grated cheese

FILLING
3 hard-boiled eggs, chopped
½ cup grated hard cheese
2 gherkins, chopped
1 teaspoon capers
3 rashers bacon, cooked and crumbled

Sift flour, salt and pepper. Rub in butter and stir in corn cereal. Mix in egg-yolk and enough cold water to make a firm dough. Roll out on floured board and cut into 2-in. circles. Spoon filling on to half circles, brush edges with egg and cover with remaining rounds, pressing edges with fork. Brush tops with egg and sprinkle with a little extra grated cheese. Cut a slit in each and bake in hot oven 18 to 20 minutes.

FILLING: Combine all ingredients well together.

Cheese Crescent

Cheese Daisies

2 tablespoons sesame seeds
6 oz. butter
1½ cups finely grated tasty cheddar cheese
¼ cup grated parmesan cheese
1½ cups plain flour
1 teaspoon salt
1 teaspoon paprika
3 tablespoons poppy seeds

Toast sesame seeds in dry pan until golden brown. Spread on plate to cool. Cream butter and grated cheeses, add sesame seeds and mix well. Sift flour, salt and paprika and add to creamed mixture. Mix thoroughly and put into biscuit press. Using a flower dish, press out on baking trays lined with quilted aluminium foil. Roll tiny balls of dough in poppy seeds for centre of each flower. Bake in moderate oven about 15 minutes. Leave to cool on baking trays.

Veal Bake with Cashew Cheese Swirls

1½ lb. veal steak, cut into serving size portions
1 egg
4 tablespoons parmesan grated cheese
½ cup plain flour, seasoned
4 tablespoons butter

SAUCE
3 tablespoons butter
3 tablespoons chopped onion
2 tablespoons chopped red or green pepper
3 tablespoons plain flour
1 teaspoon salt
1½ cups milk
1½ cups evaporated milk
2 bayleaves
1 tablespoon tomato paste

TOPPING
½ cup milk
1½ cups self-raising flour
3 oz. butter
½ teaspoon salt
pinch cayenne pepper
1 cup shredded cheddar cheese
1-1½ tablespoons anchovy sauce
4 oz. cashew nuts, roasted

Coat steaks with seasoned flour, dip in beaten egg mixed with a little water and then coat lightly with the cheese. Let stand half hour and then fry gently in hot butter until just cooked. Place in greased open oven-ware dish. Pour savoury sauce over and top with the cashew cheese swirls and bake in moderately hot oven (400°-375°) 20 minutes reducing if necessary last 10 minutes. Sprinkle with little parsley and serve hot with green bean salad.

SAUCE: Melt the butter in pan. Add onion and pepper and cook till onion is golden. Remove from heat. Blend in flour, tomato paste, and milks. Add bayleaves and salt and stir over heat until thick. Remove bayleaves.

TOPPING: Sift flour, salt, cayenne. Rub in butter and add milk. Make fairly stiff dough. Roll out on floured board about ¼-½ in. thick. Spread with anchovy sauce. Sprinkle with cheese and roughly chopped cashew nuts. Roll up like jam roll. Cut into swirls ½ in. thick and place on top of veal and sauce in dish.

Bacon and Sausage Plait

(Serves 6)

PASTRY
3 cups plain flour
½ teaspoon salt
6 oz. butter
approximately ¼ cup water

FILLING
2 hard-boiled eggs
salt, pepper
½ teaspoon powdered sage or basil
½ lb. bacon rashers
½ lb. pork sausage meat
beaten egg for glazing

PASTRY: Sift flour and salt into mixing bowl, rub in butter until mixture resembles fine breadcrumbs. Add water, mix to firm dough. Turn on to a floured board and knead well. Roll out the pastry to 10 in. square.

FILLING: Chop bacon and hard-boiled eggs, mix with remaining filling ingredients (except egg-glazing), and place down the centre of pastry. Cut pastry on each side of filling into diagonal ½-in. strips; brush with beaten egg. Lift alternate strips over the sausage mixture to form a roll resembling a plait. Brush with egg, sprinkle with a little salt. Bake in hot oven 30 to 40 minutes. (See illustration on page 14)

Corn and Bacon Pie

short pastry
½ teaspoon soft butter
8 oz. sliced bacon
1 cup chopped onion
1 cup grated cheese
2 eggs
1 large can cream-style sweet corn
freshly ground black pepper to taste
pinch cayenne
⅔ cup evaporated milk, scalded

Roll out pastry and line a 9-in. buttered pie plate. Rub inside of shell with ½ teaspoon soft butter, chill about 1 hour. Fry bacon until crisp, drain. Pour fat from pan, leaving about a tablespoon. Fry onion in this until tender. Crumble bacon, mix with onion and spread in chilled crust. Sprinkle with ½ cup cheese. Beat eggs, blend in corn, pepper and cayenne. Add remaining cheese, stir in scalded milk. Pour into pastry shell. Bake in hot oven 10 minutes. Reduce heat to moderately slow and bake 25 minutes longer. Cut in wedges and serve warm.

Veal Bake with Cashew Cheese Swirls

Crookwell Shellfish Pottle

(Serves 6-8)
1 lb. scallops
1½ lb. fresh or canned crab
2 cups dry white wine
4 cups boiling water
6 oz. butter
½ cup sherry
½ cup hot cream
1 cup plain flour
2 oz. melted butter
4 oz. artichoke (cut in quarters)
2 large lobsters
3 small onions
1 small piece celery
few parsley stalks
salt
few peppercorns
cayenne pepper
little lemon juice

PUFF PASTRY
8 oz. plain flour
8 oz. butter
1 dessertspoon finely chopped parsley and dill
5 oz. iced water
½ teaspoon salt
1 egg
1 teaspoon lemon juice

Sieve the flour and salt into a cold bowl, add lemon juice and a quarter of the butter (diced). Rub together lightly with tips of fingers until the mixture resembles fine breadcrumbs, then mix with just enough iced water to make a rather stiff dough. Turn out on to floured board and work it well until it no longer sticks to the fingers and is very smooth. Roll it rather thinly into an oblong. The remaining butter to be used should be as nearly as possible of the same consistency as the pastry; work it with the hands into a neat thin cake and place in centre of dough loosely and flatten the folds with a rolling-pin. Roll pastry into oblong strip, not allowing butter to break through. Fold dough in 3 and place, wrapped in plastic, in refrigerator 15 minutes. Remove from refrigerator, roll again and place in refrigerator again for 15 minutes. Do this once again (3 rolls in all), freezing the last time for ½ hour. Roll out into oblong strip and spread mixture of herbs on top, fold in 3, wrap and chill ½ hour. Remove from refrigerator for the last time, roll to ¼ in. thickness, cut pastry into strips ¼ in. wide, using pastry wheel. Twist each strip. Measure oval or round platter (on which food is to be served) and lay the twisted sheets of pastry on baking sheet, the same size as platter. Lay diagonal strips of pastry across the oval to make lattice of pastry. Press down well on the joints, glaze with beaten egg. Bake in hot oven 10 minutes. Reduce heat to moderately hot, bake until pastry is brown all over. Cool, loosen carefully from baking sheet and set aside.

FILLING: Wash scallops well in cold water. Place in saucepan with 1 cup white wine, 1 finely chopped onion, 1 cup water; simmer 5 minutes. Remove from saucepan and place in pan with the 2 oz. melted butter; keep warm. Remove claws from lobsters and cook claws in 1 cup white wine, remaining water, and vegetables and peppercorns; simmer gently about 15 minutes. Remove tail meat from lobsters, cut into even slices, remove claw and body meat, and reserve any coral. Place lobster meat in pan with the scallops and melted butter; add drained crabmeat, if possible in chunks, not flaked; keep warm. In top of double boiler melt 6 oz. butter, stir in flour. Cook slowly a minute or so, but don't colour. Slowly stir in 4 cups strained broth from scallops and lobster claws, stir until it comes to boil. Place pan over gently boiling water about 20 minutes, then strain into bowl. Take a little of the sauce and mix with the reserved coral until smooth. Mix with sherry, salt, pepper, lemon juice to taste. Add to sauce. Carefully mix in the artichoke hearts, cream and the combined seafood. Place on shallow platter that pastry strips were measured on, and arrange latticed pastry strips on top. Place lobster claws in several openings of the lattice. If any puff pastry remains, roll out and, with fancy cutter, cut into small crescents. Or the pastry can be cut into small rounds. Bake in hot oven with the pastry lattice shell. Surround completed seafood platter with the little pastry crescents.

Yoghurt Chicken Casserole

(Serves 6)
2 small chickens
salt and pepper
1 cup plain flour
3 oz. butter
2 large onions, sliced
2 cups water
2 chicken bouillon cubes
2 cups yoghurt
paprika

Cut each chicken into 6 pieces. Toss in paper bag with flour, seasoned with salt and pepper. Melt butter in frypan, add chicken and brown on all sides. Put in casserole with sliced onions. Sprinkle over remaining flour from paper bag, add water in which chicken bouillon cubes have been dissolved, cover and bake in moderately slow oven for 1 hour or until chicken is tender. Ten minutes before serving remove lid, add yoghurt and sprinkle with paprika.

Crab and Mushroom Quiche

(Serves 6 as main dish; 12 as entrée)
1½ cups plain flour
¼ teaspoon salt
4 oz. butter

FILLING
4 oz. fresh mushrooms, peeled and sliced
1 teaspoon butter
4 oz. gruyère cheese, finely diced
1 cup crabmeat
¾ cup sour cream
cream
¼ cup mayonnaise
3 eggs, lightly beaten
⅛ teaspoon tabasco
2 tablespoons finely chopped parsley

Mix 2 tablespoons of the flour with 2 or 3 tablespoons of cold water, stir until smooth, set aside. Sift remaining flour with salt into bowl, cut in the butter with 2 knives until the mixture forms coarse crumbs. Add the flour/water mixture, stirring with a fork, pressing down the dough until it begins to hold together. Gather dough in hands and form a ball. Chill until ready to use. Roll out pastry to a circle about 10½ in. in diameter. Gently ease the pastry into 9½-in. pie plate and trim ½ in. beyond rim of plate, turn under the overhanging edge, flute edge with fingers. Prick the surface with a fork, bake in a very hot oven 10 minutes. Cool while preparing the filling.

FILLING: Sauté the mushrooms in the butter 2 minutes, scatter them over the partially baked crust with the cheese and crabmeat. Combine the sour cream and mayonnaise with enough cream to measure 2 cups of liquid. Blend in the eggs, tabasco and parsley, pour into crust. Bake in moderate oven 50 minutes or until set. Serve hot.

Black-Eyed Beef and Husk Salad

(Serves 4)
2-2½ lb. eye fillet of beef (in one piece)
4 oz. butter
3 tablespoons plain flour
¼ lb. bacon
salt, pepper
1 dozen prunes
1 cup dry white wine
1 lb. puff pastry
1 egg-yolk
1 beef stock cube

HUSK SALAD
2 pineapples
4 oz. ham
1 cup croûtons
1 tomato
1 tablespoon grated cheese
1 small red pepper
salad dressing
salt, pepper

Remove any fat on the fillet. Insert a long, thin carving knife in the centre of the fillet, making a tunnel from one end to the other (by twisting the knife round until it penetrates). Remove rind from bacon. Chop bacon finely, combine with seeded, chopped prunes. Fill into tunnel in the meat. Combine flour, salt and pepper to taste, rub well into the fillet. Dot freely with lumps of butter. Place into baking dish and cook in hot oven until the fillet has browned well all over (approximately 10 to 15 minutes). Add wine and cook further 5 minutes; allow to cool. Reserve pan juices. When fillet has cooled sufficiently, encase it in the rolled-out puff pastry, glaze with beaten egg-yolk. Place fillet into the clean baking dish, bake in very hot oven approximately 20 minutes until the pastry shell has turned golden brown. When cooked, place meat on to serving dish, cut into 1-in. slices and coat freely with Butter Sauce.

BUTTER SAUCE: To the pan juices which have been reserved, add 1 cup beef stock (made from stock cube). Cook, stirring constantly, until sauce begins to thicken. Serve immediately.

HUSK SALAD: Cut pineapples in halves lengthwise, right through crown. Remove flesh, core and cut into cubes; reserve shells. In mixing bowl place lettuce torn into bite-sized pieces, ham cut into thin strips, cheese, tomato cut into wedges, and croûtons (small bread cubes fried until crisp in butter). Gently add salad dressing, and salt and pepper to taste; mix. Add pineapple cubes. Arrange into each pineapple shell and decorate with strips of red pepper.

Pork Fillet

(Serves 3-4)
6 oz. dried apricots
1 cup dry red wine
few blanched almonds
1 lb. pork fillet
3 oz. butter
4 tablespoons chopped onions
2 oz. bacon
1 cup beef stock
2 tablespoons tomato sauce
½ teaspoon cumin
salt, pepper
little water
3 tablespoons plain flour
1 cup sour cream

Soak apricots in wine 2 to 3 hours, then cook in wine until soft; add almonds. Cut fillet into medium slices. Pound with mallet, season with salt and pepper. Fry in butter on both sides until just done (5 to 6 minutes). Keep hot on a serving dish. Fry onions and chopped bacon lightly, add beef stock, tomato sauce, cumin and the flour, which has been blended with a little water. Cook gently until thick, stir in sour cream, salt and pepper. Pour sauce over fillets. Serve with the apricots as garnish.

Governor's Lady Devilled Crab

1 lb. cooked crabmeat
2 teaspoons lemon juice
2 teaspoons worcestershire sauce
8 oz. butter
2 tablespoons plain flour
1 teaspoon prepared mustard
¼ cup milk
1 cup cream
salt, pepper
6 large square cracker biscuits
parsley
lemon wedges

Combine crabmeat, lemon juice and worcestershire sauce in basin. Melt 6 oz. butter in saucepan, stir in flour and mustard, cook 1 minute over low heat; gradually add milk and cream. Cook, stirring continually, over low heat until thick. Remove from heat, stir in crabmeat, season to taste; mix well. Place mixture into 4 buttered crab shells or ramekins. Crush biscuits finely, stir in remaining melted butter, mixing well. Sprinkle over crab mixture. Bake in hot oven 15 minutes. Garnish with parsley and lemon wedges.

Black-Eyed Beef and Husk Salad

Seafood Banquet Pie

2 eggs, beaten
½ cup milk
2 tablespoons melted butter
1 small chopped onion
2 tablespoons finely chopped parsley
¾ teaspoon basil
¼ teaspoon salt
15 oz. can chunk style tuna

PASTRY
8 oz. self-raising flour
½ teaspoon salt
3½ oz. butter
2-3 tablespoons cold water

CUCUMBER SAUCE
1 cup grated cucumber (cut cucumber in half lengthwise, scoop out seeds and grate, then drain)
1 small grated onion
2 tablespoons mayonnaise
2 teaspoons vinegar
1 tablespoon parsley (finely chopped or minced)
4 oz. sour cream
salt and pepper to taste

Combine eggs, milk, melted butter, onion, parsley, basil, salt and stir in tuna. Pour into 8-in. greased ovenware dish or 8-in. pie plate.

PASTRY: Sift flour and salt and cut in butter until particles are the size of small peas. Add 1 tablespoon water, gently toss with a fork. Sprinkle next tablespoon over dry part and push moistened part aside, repeat till all is moistened. Gather up with fingers and form into a ball. Flatten ball slightly and roll out $\frac{1}{8}$ in. thick on a lightly floured surface. With sharp knife cut circle using bottom of an 8-in. pie plate as guide, then cut circle into 6 pie shapeu wedges. Arrange on top of seafood mixture and bake in a moderately hot oven (425°) for about 25 minutes or until top is golden brown.

CUCUMBER SAUCE: Combine onion, mayonnaise, vinegar, parsley sour cream and salt and pepper. Then combine with grated cucumber Chill well.

Swiss Onion Pie

1½ cups plain flour
1 tablespoon cornflour
½ teaspoon salt
4 oz. butter
cold water

FILLING
3 slices bacon cut into ½-in. strips
2 oz. butter
3 medium onions, finely chopped
2 eggs
1 cup sour cream
salt and pepper
1 teaspoon chopped chives
¼ cup milk

Sift dry ingredients into bowl. Rub in butter lightly and mix with water to a firm dough. Roll out pastry and line buttered 8-in. tart plate. Chill. Pour filling into chilled pastry and bake in hot oven for 10 minutes, then reduce heat to moderate and continue baking until filling is set, approximately 20 to 30 minutes.

FILLING: Fry bacon until crisp, drain. Add butter to pan and sauté onions until tender. Beat eggs, blend in cream, bacon, onions and remaining ingredients.

Chicken Pancakes

1 cup plain flour
pinch salt
1 egg
½ pint milk
butter for frying

FILLING
8 oz. cooked chicken
2 oz. butter
½ cup plain flour
¾ pint milk
2 egg-yolks
juice and rind of ½ orange
seasoning
grated orange rind
cucumber slices

Sift flour and salt. Stir in egg and sufficient milk to form a smooth batter. Heat a little butter in frypan and pour in sufficient batter to cover base thinly. Cook over moderate heat until golden, then turn or toss and cook second side. Repeat until all batter is used. Place some filling on each pancake and roll up. Place in serving dish and pour a little of the sauce over. Serve remaining sauce separately. Garnish with orange rind and cucumber slices.

FILLING: Chop chicken. Make sauce by melting butter and stirring in flour. Add milk gradually and bring to boil, stirring all the time and cook 1 to 2 minutes. Remove from heat, cool slightly and beat in egg-yolks. Add rind and juice of orange and season to taste. Mix chicken with some of the sauce, divide between pancakes.

Gruyère Cream Tart

4 oz. self-raising flour
4 oz. plain flour
4 oz. cream cheese
4 oz. butter
¼ teaspoon salt

FILLING
8 oz. packet of sliced gruyère cheese
6 oz. cream
4 oz. smoked ham
2 tablespoons parmesan cheese
3 eggs
1 tablespoon onion juice
salt and pepper
chervil
few green and black olives

Beat together butter and cream cheese until smooth. Sift flours and salt and add to creamed mixture to make a soft dough. Roll on well-floured board to fit large shallow tart plate. Place in refrigerator while making filling. Beat together eggs, salt, pepper and onion juice. Add cream and beat lightly again. Cut sliced cheese into match-sticks. Chop ham fairly fine and spread over pastry base. Cover ham with cheese strips and carefully pour egg/cream mixture over cheese. Sprinkle parmesan gently on the top. Place tart in hot oven 450° for 10 minutes then reduce heat to 325°. Bake for about 30-40 minutes or until filling is set. When cooked sprinkle generously with chervil and garnish with sliced black and green olives. Serve with lettuce wedges and tomatoes, with french dressing and cucumber slices topped with yoghurt and sprinkled with chopped chives.

Grilled Hot Crab Sandwich with Cheese Sauce

(Serves 6)
2 oz. butter
4 tablespoons plain flour
1½ cups milk
¾ lb. sharp cheese cut into small cubes
1 tablespoon dry white wine
1 teaspoon worcestershire sauce
½ teaspoon tabasco sauce
6 slices toast cut into rounds
1½ lb. crabmeat
paprika

Melt the butter, stir in the flour; when bubbling and well blended, add the milk, stirring constantly. When the mixture is thickened and smooth, remove from heat. Add cheese, wine, worcestershire sauce and tabasco. Stir until mixture is smooth, keep hot, but do not boil. Arrange toast rounds in six individual heatproof casseroles and top the toast with equal portions of crabmeat. Spoon measures of cheese sauce over crab and then sprinkle with paprika. Grill until golden brown.

Australian Fillet

(Serves 4)
2½ lb. fillet of beef
8 oz. mushrooms, finely chopped
4-6 oz. butter
11 slices cooked ham or boiled bacon
1 egg-yolk
1 onion, finely chopped
1 clove garlic, crushed
brandy
salt, pepper
softened butter
puff pastry

BEARNAISE SAUCE
¼ cup tarragon vinegar
½ cup water
4 oz. butter
6-8 shallots, finely chopped
2 egg-yolks
salt, pepper
little lemon juice

Make 1 lb. puff pastry in usual way, using plain flour. Season fillet with garlic or wipe pan with garlic for milder flavour. Brush fillet with brandy; trim it neatly, removing ends and slice into 12 equal parts without completely separating the slices. Place a thin slice of cooked ham or boiled bacon, cut to fit the fillet, between each slice, and spread with some of the finely chopped mushrooms and onions, seasoned to taste and sautéed until soft in butter. Re-form the fillet, fasten with metal skewers, and roast in moderate oven 15 to 20 minutes or until half cooked. Allow fillet to cool slightly; remove skewers and fat; spread with softened butter; season to taste with salt and freshly ground black pepper, and spread thinly with remaining mushroom mixture. Roll out puff pastry into a thin sheet and wrap the fillet in it, securing it neatly. Place on a baking sheet; brush pastry with cold water, bake in hot oven 12 to 15 minutes. Brush the pastry with slightly beaten egg-yolk and continue baking until the crust is browned. Serve on a heated plate. Serve with Bearnaise Sauce, sauté potatoes, carrots and green beans.

BEARNAISE SAUCE: Boil the shallots in the vinegar and water until liquid is reduced by two-thirds. Now place them either in the top of a double boiler or in a basin over hot water, stir in the well-beaten egg-yolks, and add the butter in small pieces, stirring steadily all the time as sauce thickens. Season to taste; gradually stir in the lemon juice. Sieve the sauce, add a little chopped chervil and tarragon, and serve.

Australian Seafood and Avocado

(Serves 6-8)
1 lb. cooked prawns, shelled
1 lb. cooked crabmeat, flaked
1 lb. cooked fresh scallops
3 ripe avocados
1 cup diced fresh mushrooms
1 onion, finely chopped
3 tablespoons tomato purée
1 cup cream
1 cup dry white wine
6 tablespoons butter
4 tablespoons plain flour
juice 1 lemon
1 large can oyster soup
1 tablespoon curry powder
1 teaspoon paprika
1 bayleaf
salt, pepper

Melt 4 tablespoons butter, blend in flour, and gradually add oyster soup. Stir and cook 5 minutes until mixture thickens, then simmer 5 minutes. In another pan, melt 2 tablespoons butter, sauté the chopped onion and mushrooms. When these are lightly coloured, add to the oyster sauce and blend in the curry powder, paprika, tomato purée, cream and white wine. Fold in seafood mixture, add bayleaf; simmer while preparing the avocados. Halve the avocados, remove stone and flesh from shell in one piece. Then slice flesh into lengthwise strips. Sprinkle with salt and lemon juice to preserve colour. Add avocado to seafood, stirring in gently. Transfer all to a lightly buttered casserole. Bake in slow oven 20 minutes. Serve immediately with a green salad with french dressing, boiled rice and a chilled dry white wine.

Grilled Hot Crab Sandwich with Cheese Sauce

Roast Pork Capricornia

(Serves 6)
3-3½ lb. loin pork with rind scored
1 small lemon
1 cup burgundy
olive oil
water, salt

SAUCE
½ cup brandy
½ cup seeded raisins
6 (or more) canned peach halves
½ cup juice from canned peaches
2 medium sized oranges
1 green pepper
3 cloves garlic
½ lb. firm white mushrooms
5 oz. butter
1 tablespoon plain flour
2 firm tomatoes
1 cup chicken stock
2 tablespoons red currant jelly
1 dessertspoon tomato paste
1 dessertspoon beef extract
water, salt

Preheat oven to hot. Rub meat all over with lemon juice. Dry off excess juice and rub well with salt. Brush olive oil over rind. Put loin into small roasting pan and pour in 2 tablespoons each of water and burgundy. Place in oven and reduce heat immediately to moderately hot. Roast 1½ to 2 hours, basting every 20 minutes. After each basting, add to pan 1 tablespoon each of burgundy and water. While meat is roasting, make the sauce.

SAUCE: Soak the raisins in ¼ cup brandy. Wash mushrooms, peel and cut stalks short. Slice 4 mushrooms thickly. Remove seeds from pepper, slice thinly. Chop garlic finely. Peel oranges carefully and slice rind in long, very thin strips. Separate orange segments, place in bowl, sprinkle with remainder of brandy and allow to stand. Skin tomatoes and slice fairly thickly. Heat 3 oz. butter in large pan, add orange rind and garlic. Cook slowly 6 minutes, stirring occasionally. Remove pan from heat and stir in tomato paste, beef extract, red currant jelly, chicken stock, peach syrup and plain flour which has been mixed with a little water. Return mixture to the heat and stir until boiling, then add sliced mushrooms, pepper, tomatoes, raisins and brandy. Simmer gently 5 or 6 minutes, then add the orange segments and brandy. Add salt to taste. Keep sauce hot.

TO SERVE: In another pan sauté 6 mushrooms whole (more if extra peaches used) in 2 oz. butter until tender. Remove mushrooms and keep warm. Heat peaches in the same butter. When roast is ready, remove from oven and place on hot platter. Surround with peaches with a mushroom in centre of each. Pour hot sauce over all.

Tenderloin Australian

(Serves 4)
1 whole eye fillet of beef
clarified butter for frying

BASTING MARINADE
2 tablespoons red wine
2 tablespoons clarified butter
1 tablespoon wine vinegar
1 teaspoon dry mustard
1 teaspoon salt
little ground black pepper
little garlic salt

SAUCE
1 tablespoon butter
4 tablespoons flour
¼ pint cream
¼ pint milk
3 tablespoons chopped parsley mixed with chopped chives
2 king prawns, peeled and chopped
1 small chicken breast
1 egg, separated
few drops lemon juice
salt, pepper

Mix together in a small bowl all the ingredients for basting marinade. Heat clarified butter in frypan until very hot. Brown the fillet all over, as quickly as possible, to seal in the juices. Then reduce heat, baste regularly and on all sides with the basting marinade. A pastry brush made of bristle is ideal for this purpose. Cook 20-40 minutes on a low heat, depending on whether taste runs to rare, medium or well done. Make a slit along the whole length of the fillet, cutting down halfway; turn fillet open and keep hot.

SAUCE: Melt the butter in a saucepan, but do not brown, add the flour and cook 1 minute. Add the cream and milk all at once and bring to the boil, stirring continually; add salt and pepper to taste. Add chopped prawns and cooked chopped chicken breast, heat through. Add chopped parsley and chives, carefully add beaten egg-yolk, then a few drops of lemon juice. Finally, lightly fold in the stiffly beaten egg-white. Spread this sauce mixture all along the slit in the fillet and brown quickly under very hot griller.

TO SERVE: Serve with very small new potatoes which have been cooked in a steamer until almost done, then fried in very hot butter 10 minutes, tossing all the time. Sprinkle salt and black pepper on them while frying.

TOMATO BASKETS WITH PEAS: Halve large tomatoes, hollow out centre. Put tomato halves in steamer so they can heat through without losing their shape. Mix hot cooked peas with a tablespoon of bottled sauce tartare and spoon into hot tomato halves.

Beef Goulash with Dumplings

(Serves 6)
1 onion, chopped
1 green pepper, chopped
1 clove garlic, minced
4 oz. butter
2 lb. chuck or oyster blade steak, cubed
½ cup plain flour
salt and pepper
1½ cups hot water
2 bouillon cubes
few drops tabasco sauce
1 teaspoon paprika
1 teaspoon salt
¼ teaspoon pepper
1 cup evaporated milk
1 dessertspoon lemon juice
1½ cups diced carrots
1½ cups green beans

DUMPLINGS
1½ cups self-raising flour
½ teaspoon salt
½ teaspoon caraway seeds
2 oz. butter
cold water to mix

Sauté onion, pepper and garlic in butter until soft and lightly browned. Remove and in remaining butter in pan brown the meat tossed in seasoned flour. Return onion mixture and water with dissolved bouillon cubes, and seasonings. Cover and simmer 1½ hours. Add evaporated milk previously soured with lemon juice, carrots and beans. Cover and simmer 25 minutes or until vegetables are tender. Drop dumpling mixture in tablespoonsful on top of meat. Cover and simmer 15 to 18 minutes longer.

DUMPLINGS: Mix dry ingredients with caraway seeds, rub in butter and mix to a firm, light dough with water.

Golden Mornay Puff

7 oz. plain flour
4 oz. butter
2 egg-yolks
¼ cup finely grated cheddar cheese
1 cup water
4 oz. butter
1 cup plain flour
pinch salt
4 eggs
¼ cup finely grated cheddar cheese
1 cup shelled, cooked prawns
6 large fillets of sole or flounder
1 cup water, boiled
1 cup white wine
1 teaspoon salt
2 cups cooked, well-drained and chopped spinach
½ cup minced or finely chopped ham
¼ cup grated cheddar cheese
1 teaspoon onion juice
salt and pepper
2 tablespoons finely chopped shallots
asparagus spears

WINE SAUCE
3 dessertspoons melted butter
3 dessertspoons plain flour
½ teaspoon salt
½ teaspoon mustard
1 cup grated cheddar cheese
½ teaspoon worcestershire sauce

POTATO PUFFS
½ cup creamy mashed potato
oil for frying

Sift flour into a basin. Rub in butter. Add egg-yolks and cheese. Mix thoroughly. Roll out on a lightly-floured board to a 10-in. circle. Place on an oven slide and chill. Heat water and butter until boiling. Add one cup plain flour and salt all at once, stir until mixture leaves sides of saucepan and forms a ball. Cool slightly. Beat in eggs and cheddar cheese. Pipe around edge of 10-in. pastry circle. Reserve remaining paste for Potato Puffs. Bake at 400° for 25-35 minutes, until puff is well risen and golden. Sprinkle prawns (keep few for garnish) over fillets. Roll up fillets and secure with cotton or a toothpick. Boil water, white wine and salt. Add fish fillets and simmer for about 7 minutes or until tender. Lift out fish fillets and keep hot. Reserve liquid. Combine spinach, ham, cheese, onion juice and salt and pepper. Spoon over base of cooked pie shell. Arrange fish fillets in wheel spokes on top of spinach. Pour sauce generously over individual fish pieces. Bake at 400° for 10 minutes until topping is golden brown. Garnish with chopped reserved prawns, sprinkle with shallots. Arrange asparagus spears between fish (heat asparagus in its own liquid).

WINE SAUCE: Melt butter and blend in flour, salt and mustard. Cook until bubbly, remove from heat and stir in 1¼ cups of the water-wine liquid from the fish. Cook and stir until thickened. Add 1 cup grated cheese and worcestershire sauce and cook stirring 5 minutes or until cheese has melted.

POTATO PUFFS: Blend mashed potato well with leftover paste and mix well. Drop very small spoonsful into deep hot oil. Cook for few minutes until puffs are golden. Drain. Pile on to a plate.

Pork with Piquant Fruit Sauce

(Serves 4)
1 lb. slice of middle-cut leg pork
10 dried apricots or nectarines
6 rashers bacon
1 tablespoon plain flour
1 tablespoon cornflour
2 eggs
¼ teaspoon monosodium glutamate
salt, pepper

PIQUANT FRUIT SAUCE
½ cup tomato sauce
2 dessertspoons melted butter
2 cloves garlic
½ green pepper
½ red pepper
1 large onion
1 ripe firm tomato
1 small can pineapple pieces
water
1 tablespoon sugar
1 dessertspoon cider vinegar
salt to taste
¼ teaspoon monosodium glutamate
1 dessertspoon cornflour

Cut pork into 1-in. cubes and slit each cube to form a pocket. Soak apricots or nectarines in boiling water to cover until soft. Strain and mince or chop very finely. Stuff into pockets in meat cubes. Remove rind from bacon, cut each rasher in half lengthwise. Cut into strips to equal the number of pork cubes; wrap a bacon strip round each pork cube. Mix flour and cornflour with the seasonings, then stir in the beaten eggs; whip until batter is light. Dip each cube in the batter until well coated and fry in deep fat until golden brown. Place on a platter and keep warm while preparing the Piquant Fruit Sauce.

PIQUANT FRUIT SAUCE: Mince garlic finely, cut peppers into squares. Cut onion in two horizontally, then into wedges; skin tomato, cut into wedges. Drain pineapple pieces, reserving syrup. Set aside a little syrup to blend cornflour to a paste, make up remainder of syrup with cold water to ¾ cup of liquid. Heat butter, brown the garlic, add peppers, then the other prepared vegetables. Fry a little, then add all remaining ingredients except cornflour. Simmer 5 minutes, then add cornflour blended with syrup. Simmer, stirring, until thickened. Pour this sauce over the hot fried pork cubes, dust with paprika and serve hot.

Cheese Crumble Spaghetti Loaf

1¼ cups cream
3 tablespoons butter
1¼ cups dry breadcrumbs
½ teaspoon dried thyme
1 teaspoon salt
¾ cup grated cheddar cheese
4 eggs
1 tablespoon grated onion
2½ tablespoons finely chopped green pepper
1½ tablespoons finely chopped parsley
¾ cup cooked spaghetti

CHEESE CRUST
1½ tablespoons butter
1 cup (4 oz.) plain flour
½ cup grated cheddar cheese
¼ teaspoon pimento
pinch black pepper

CHEESE AND MUSHROOM SAUCE
1 small onion
1½ tablespoons butter
8 oz. can mushrooms
1 tablespoon plain flour
½ cup cream
¾ cup grated cheddar cheese
¼ teaspoon salt
pepper

Heat cream and butter until butter melts. Pour over breadcrumbs, thyme and salt. Stand ten minutes. Add cheese, well beaten eggs, onion, green pepper, parsley and spaghetti. Mix well. Pour into a loaf tin lined with foil. Cover with Cheese Crust. Place loaf tin in baking dish half full of water. Bake in moderate oven (350°G, 375°E) 1 hour. Remove from oven and cool two or three minutes. Lift out and serve with Cheese and Mushroom Sauce.

CHEESE CRUST: Rub butter into sifted flour. Add cheese, pimento and pinch black pepper. Mix together using residue of beaten egg.

SAUCE: Lightly sauté finely sliced onion in butter. Add mushrooms, cover and simmer till tender. Blend in flour. Add cream. Stir gently to blend. Cook until thickened. Add cheese, salt and pinch pepper. Stir and cook until cheese is melted.

Pork with Piquant Fruit Sau

Cheese and Cucumber Tart

6 oz. self-raising flour
2 oz. plain flour
¼ level teaspoon salt
4 oz. butter
¾ cup crushed walnuts
5 tablespoons cold water
2 eggs
8 oz. grated tasty cheese
1 teaspoon salt
cayenne (pinch)
4 tablespoons grated cucumber
½ onion grated
1 cup evaporated milk diluted with ½ cup water
2 oz. butter

Sift flours and salt. Rub in butter. Add crushed nuts, then add water, stir quickly and lightly. Roll out and line a tart plate. Beat eggs well, add cheese, salt, cayenne, grated cucumber, onion, milk and melted butter. Pour mixture into pastry shell and cook in a hot oven 450° for 8 minutes. Reduce heat to 350°, cook gently until custard sets, about 35 to 45 minutes. Serve hot with grilled bacon rolls, peas and tomatoes.

Chicken Pie with Crunchy Cheese Topping

1 cup plain flour
½ teaspoon baking powder
½ teaspoon salt
pinch cayenne
1 cup crushed corn cereal
3 oz. butter
½ cup finely grated cheese
1 egg-yolk
1 dessertspoon lemon juice
1 tablespoon cold water

FILLING
2 oz. butter
1-2 teaspoons curry powder
2 tablespoons flour
1 8-oz. can cream of chicken soup
1¾ cups milk
salt and freshly ground pepper to taste
3 tablespoons crushed potato crisps
1½ cups diced cooked chicken

Sift flour, baking powder, salt and cayenne. Stir in cereal. Rub in butter, add cheese and then form a dough with egg-yolk beaten with lemon juice and cold water. Chill 30 minutes. Turn on to floured board, knead lightly and roll out ⅔ of pastry to fit an ovenproof dish. Roll out remaining pastry and cut into 2-in. circles. Chill. Bake pastry lined dish in hot oven 12 minutes, spoon in the filling and place chilled pastry rounds on top. Bake further 20 minutes in hot oven until hot and pastry is golden.

FILLING: Heat butter and cook curry powder 1 minute. Stir in flour, then gradually add soup and milk. Return to heat and stir until mixture boils and thickens. Season. Add crushed potato crisps and chicken, heat through.

Braised Steak and Caraway Pie

1½ cups plain flour
pinch salt
3 oz. butter
¾ cup finely shredded processed cheese
pinch caraway seeds
¼ cup water

FILLING
1 16-oz. can braised steak and onions
1 small carrot, sliced and cooked
¼ cup each chopped celery and diced parsnip, cooked

Sift flour and salt into basin, rub in butter and add cheese and caraway seeds. Gradually blend in water, adding more if necessary to make a firm dough. Knead lightly on floured board. Chill 30 minutes. Halve. Roll one half out and line a buttered 8-in. pie plate. Roll out remaining pastry to fit top and cut a cross in centre. Spoon filling into pastry lined plate and cover with pastry top. Crimp edge and bake in moderately hot oven 40 to 45 minutes until pastry is golden.

FILLING: Combine braised steak and onions and cooked vegetables.

Cheese and Cucumber Tart

Lamb Rolls Billabong

(Serves 6)
12 lamb chops
6 rashers bacon
1 egg
12 pineapple rings
plain flour
breadcrumbs
cooking oil

SAUCE SUPREME
4 oz. mushrooms
1 cup canned tomato soup
¼ cup dry white wine
½ cup cream
1 tablespoon butter
½ cup finely chopped shallots
1 chicken cube
black pepper

Remove bones from chops. Trim and shape each chop into a round. Wrap ½ rasher bacon round each, then secure with small wooden stick. Dip each into flour, then beaten egg and breadcrumbs. Brush with oil. Place on oven tray and bake in moderate oven 15 to 20 minutes. Serve each lamb roll on a ring of pineapple and garnish with parsley. Serve with green peas, duchesse potatoes, glazed carrot straws and Sauce Supreme.

SAUCE SUPREME: Fry sliced mushrooms with crumbled chicken cube in butter about 5 minutes. Add shallots, soup and wine, season with black pepper. Simmer 20 minutes. Add cream and serve.

Potato Crust Veal Pie

2 veal knuckles
1 teaspoon salt
1 small onion
½ stick celery
½ carrot
juice of 1 lemon
rind of ½ lemon
3 slices bacon
3 eggs

POTATO PASTRY
4 oz. butter
1½ cups plain flour
3 oz. cooked sieved potatoes
1 tablespoon cold water
egg or milk for glazing

Put veal, salt, onion, celery and carrot in saucepan, cover with cold water and simmer gently 1½ to 2 hours. Strain stock into basin, add lemon juice and rind. Discard vegetables. Remove meat from bones and cut into pieces. Fry bacon lightly and drain on absorbent paper. Hard boil eggs and slice.

PASTRY: Rub butter into flour. Add sieved potato. Mix to a firm dough with water. Knead until smooth. Line a deep, 7-in. pie dish with thin layer of pastry. Fill lined pie plate with layers of meat, bacon and sliced hard-boiled eggs. Cover with remaining pastry. Make a hole in centre. Glaze with egg or milk. Bake in a hot oven for 10 minutes, reduce heat to moderate and continue baking further 30 to 35 minutes or until cooked. When cold remove pie from dish. Fill with veal stock through centre hole. Allow stock to set. Serve cold.

Cheddar Chicken

(Serves 6)
1 3-lb. chicken cut into serving pieces
¼ cup flour
salt and pepper to season
4 oz. butter
1½ cups self-raising flour
1 teaspoon salt
3 egg-yolks
1½ cups milk
3 oz. melted butter
1¼ cups cheddar cheese, grated
3 egg-whites

MUSHROOM SAUCE
4 oz. mushrooms, peeled and sliced finely
2 tablespoons flour
1½ cups chicken stock
salt and pepper to season
1 cup cream

Coat chicken with flour mixed with salt and pepper. Melt 4 oz. butter in frypan over moderate heat and cook chicken, turning pieces until brown on both sides, about 15 to 20 minutes. Put into oven to keep warm. Reserve drippings. Sift self-raising flour and salt. Make well in centre. Beat egg-yolks and add milk. Stir in flour and salt. Add 3 oz. melted butter and mix until smooth. Fold in cheese and stiffly beaten egg-whites. Pour into buttered, ovenproof dish and arrange chicken pieces on top. Bake in moderately hot oven 50 to 60 minutes.

MUSHROOM SAUCE: Pour butter drippings from chicken into frypan. Add mushrooms and cook gently until tender. Remove mushrooms and put aside. To drippings in pan add flour and cook over low heat 2 to 3 minutes, stirring. Gradually add stock and cook, stirring, until smooth. Season and add cooked mushrooms. Bring to boil. Add cream and re-heat without boiling. Serve hot with chicken.

Lamb Rolls Billabong

Savoury Pancake Bake

1½ cups (6 oz.) plain flour
½ pint milk
3 eggs separated
salt
2 oz. butter

FILLING
2 oz. rice
4 oz. butter
4 oz. can mushrooms
4 oz. prepared peas
10 oz. veal
8 oz. cauliflower

SAUCE
½ cup cream
¼ cup lemon juice
2 egg-yolks

Mix flour with milk. Add egg-yolks and salt, then stiffly beaten egg-whites. Heat frypan, grease with butter and pour in a thin layer of batter mixture. Fry six pancakes on both sides a golden colour.

FILLING: Cook rice in boiling salted water. Drain. Add 1 teaspoon butter. Add 1 oz. butter to mushrooms. Add 1 teaspoon butter to prepared peas. Fry diced veal in 2 oz. butter. Cook cauliflower in salted water. Add ½ oz. butter. Butter a casserole dish and place a pancake on bottom. Spread with cooked rice. Place second pancake on top of the rice and spread with the prepared mushrooms. Place third pancake on top and cover with prepared peas. Cover with next pancake and spread with veal. Cover with pancake and spread with cauliflower. Lastly, place sixth pancake over and pour the prepared sauce on top. Bake 30 minutes in a moderate oven (350°G, 375°E). Any vegetables in season may be used and left over meat may also be used.

SAUCE: Mix cream, lemon juice and egg-yolks together.

Savoury Pie with Cheese Meringue

short pastry

FILLING
1 oz. butter
3 tablespoons plain flour
½ pint milk
1 cup grated cheddar cheese
2 egg-yolks
salt
pinch cayenne pepper
8 oz. white onions, sliced and sautéed in little butter, or 1 tin sardines

CHEESE MERINGUE
2 egg-whites
salt,
3 tablespoons grated cheddar cheese

Roll pastry out to ⅛-in. thickness and line an 8-in. buttered pie plate. Prick well. Line pastry case with paper and fill with rice or bread crusts. Bake in moderately hot oven 15 minutes, remove paper and rice and continue baking 10 minutes with temperature reduced to moderate. Spoon in filling. Cover with cheese meringue and return to oven to heat filling and set meringue.

FILLING: Melt butter, add flour and cook 1 minute. Add milk and stir until boiling. Cook 2 to 3 minutes. Add egg-yolks and cook without boiling 2 minutes. Mix in cheese, sardines or onions, salt and cayenne pepper.

CHEESE MERINGUE: Whisk egg-whites and salt until stiff. Spread over filling and sprinkle with cheese.

Cheese Tomato Pie

1¾ cups plain flour
½ teaspoon salt
1 cup grated sharp cheese
4 oz. butter
about ¼ cup iced water
egg to glaze

FILLING
3 oz. butter
1 clove garlic, crushed
6 ripe tomatoes, sliced
½ teaspoon dried basil leaves
1 tablespoon lemon juice
salt and freshly ground pepper
pinch cinnamon

Sift flour and salt. Add cheese, toss in lightly with fork. Cut in butter, using a pastry blender or 2 knives until mixture resembles breadcrumbs. Quickly sprinkle water, 1 dessertspoon at a time over pastry mixture, tossing with fork to make a firm dough. Chill 1 hour. Divide into halves. Roll out half pastry to fit a buttered 8-in. pie plate or flan ring. Spoon filling into pie case, sprinkle with cinnamon. Roll out remaining pastry to fit top. Brush edges with egg to seal. Crimp and cut a few slits to allow steam to escape. Bake in hot oven 10 minutes, lower heat to moderate and bake further 20 minutes.

FILLING: Melt butter and add garlic, then tomatoes and cook 1 minute only. Sprinkle with basil and lemon juice. Season to taste with salt and pepper.

Family Open House Pie

(Serves 6-8)
1 can refrigerated scones
(country style or buttermilk)
1 tablespoon melted butter
2 oz. butter
½ green pepper, chopped
1 medium onion, chopped
2 rashers bacon, chopped roughly
salt, pepper to taste
oregano to taste
3 medium tomatoes, skinned
1 teaspoon sugar
6 slices tasty cheese
1 tablespoon chopped parsley
1 tablespoon capers

Flatten scones to $\frac{1}{4}$ in. thick. Arrange over base and sides of 10-in. pie plate, pressing together to form a pie case. Brush with melted butter. Melt butter in frypan, sauté chopped pepper, chopped onion and chopped bacon for 2 minutes. Add seasoning, skinned, chopped tomatoes and sugar. Simmer 5 minutes. Drain a little and spoon into pie case. Bake in hot oven for 10 minutes, reduce temperature to moderate and continue baking further 15 to 20 minutes. Remove from oven, arrange cheese slices on top and return to oven to melt cheese. Sprinkle with parsley and capers. Serve hot, cut into slices.

Kidney Savoury Inverell

4 sheep's kidneys
2 bacon rashers
1 dessertspoon grated onion
1 tablespoon butter
1 medium tomato
½ cup water
1 tablespoon worcestershire sauce
1 tablespoon tomato sauce
¼ teaspoon salt
¼ teaspoon black pepper
1 teaspoon sugar
1 teaspoon vinegar or lemon juice
1 dessertspoon plain flour
1 tablespoon chopped parsley

Remove skin and core from kidneys, chop finely. Fry finely chopped bacon and onion in hot butter in pan until brown, add skinned, chopped tomato, water and chopped kidney. Season with salt and pepper and simmer slowly for 20 minutes or until tender. Blend sauces and vinegar into flour, add sugar and parsley and stir gently into kidney mixture. Stir until mixture thickens. Serve as a filling for pancakes made from a favourite recipe, as a filling for omelettes, or topping for savoury waffles. Recipe makes enough filling for 4 pancakes.

Apple Lamb Casserole

(Serves 4)
2 oz. butter
1 lb. lamb shoulder, cubed
2 tablespoons plain flour
2 cups water
1 bayleaf
1 teaspoon salt
pinch thyme, sage or rosemary
pepper to taste
1 small onion
3 cups apples, peeled and sliced
2 tablespoons lemon juice
1 cup water
2 tablespoons sugar

SCONE TOPPING
1½ cups self-raising flour
½ teaspoon salt
½ teaspoon curry powder
½ teaspoon turmeric
2 oz. butter
1 egg
⅓ cup milk

Melt butter in pan, add lamb and brown well. Sprinkle with flour, stir to coat meat, then stir in 2 cups water, bayleaf, salt, thyme, sage, pepper and onion. Cover and cook 1½ to 2 hours until meat is tender. Stir occasionally. Remove bayleaf and onion. Prepare sliced apples and sprinkle with lemon juice. Add 1 cup water, sugar and apple to meat mixture. Cook, stirring occasionally until apples are tender, about 15 to 20 minutes. Turn on to shallow baking dish. Top hot mixture with scone topping. Bake in hot oven 12 to 15 minutes.

SCONE TOPPING: Sift together flour, turmeric, salt and curry powder into mixing bowl. Cut in butter. Combine egg, milk, and add to dry ingredients. Mix lightly and knead on floured board. Roll out to ½-in. thickness and cut with round cutter into 2-in. circles.

Ham-Asparagus Bake

2 oz. butter
2 tablespoons plain flour
½ cup evaporated milk
1 15½-oz. can asparagus, drained
¼ cup asparagus liquid
salt
pepper
2 eggs, separated
8 oz. cooked ham, cut into ½-in. cubes

SAVOURY BISCUITS
1 cup plain flour
3 oz. butter
2-3 tablespoons prepared sandwich spread
½ cup grated cheddar
melted butter

Melt butter in saucepan, stir in flour off the heat until smooth. Add evaporated milk and asparagus liquid, bring to boil, stirring all the time. Cook 3 minutes. Season with salt and pepper and stir through lightly beaten egg-yolks. Fold in asparagus and ham. Beat egg-whites stiffly and fold through mixture. Put in buttered casserole dish or ramekins. Bake in hot oven 15 to 20 minutes.

SAVOURY BISCUITS: Sift flour into bowl and work butter in until dough is formed. Knead and roll out on lightly floured board. Cut into triangles and place half on oven slide. Spread with sandwich spread. Cover with remaining biscuits, brush with melted butter, sprinkle with cheese. Bake on top shelf of hot oven with casserole on lower shelf.

Kidney Savoury Inverell

Chicken Paprika

1 3-lb. chicken disjointed
the giblets
2 cups water
1 small onion, halved
2 teaspoons salt
4 whole peppercorns
1 bayleaf
1 small onion, finely chopped
3 oz. butter
1 cup plain flour
6 teaspoons paprika
⅓ cup cream
⅓ cup strong black coffee
1½ cups sour cream

Put giblets, neck and feet in saucepan with water, halved onion, half the salt, peppercorns and bayleaf. Simmer, covered 1 hour. Sauté chopped onion in 1 oz. butter until soft but not brown. Remove onion, leaving butter in frypan. Combine flour, reserving 1 tablespoon for later use, remaining salt and 2 teaspoons paprika in a paper bag. Shake chicken pieces in bag until coated with flour mixture. Brown well in butter in pan. Add ¼ cup giblet broth and cook, covered, over low heat until chicken is tender, about 30 to 40 minutes. Heat remaining butter in saucepan, blend in reserved flour. Add giblet broth, chopped giblets, cream, coffee and remaining paprika. Stir over low heat until smooth and thickened. Add sour cream gradually, stirring vigorously. Pour sauce over chicken in pan and cook over low heat 3 minutes, turning chicken and stirring sauce. Do not boil.

Veal and Bacon Casserole

8 oz. bacon rashers, diced
1 lb. lean veal steak, cut into 1-in. cubes
2 tablespoons plain flour
salt and pepper
3 oz. butter
1 lb. tomatoes, peeled
¼ cup water
1 cup grated cheese

DUMPLINGS
1 cup self-raising flour
1 teaspoon curry powder
½ teaspoon salt
1 oz. butter
milk to mix

Toss bacon and veal in seasoned flour. Heat butter and sauté veal and bacon until brown on all sides. Put into casserole, cover with sliced tomatoes, pour water over and top with cheese. Cover and bake in moderate oven about 1 hour. Arrange dumplings on top, return to hot oven and cook uncovered 15 minutes or until golden.

DUMPLINGS: Sift flour, curry powder and salt. Rub in butter and stir in enough milk to make a soft dough. Knead gently on floured board. Pat out to ½-in. thickness, cut into shapes.

Savoury Cheese and Butter Suzettes

4 eggs
1 pint milk
2 cups plain flour
½ teaspoon salt
extra 2 tablespoons flour
1¼ lb. minced steak
2 oz. butter
1 onion, grated
1 clove garlic, crushed
¾ teaspoon salt
pepper to taste
1 cup tomato purée
parsley to garnish

CHEESE SAUCE
2 oz. butter
2 tablespoons flour
½ pint milk
salt and pepper to taste
1 cup grated cheese

Beat eggs, add ½ pint milk and mix in 2 cups flour and salt. Beat until smooth. Add remaining milk gradually. Grease a small hot pan with butter and pour in just enough batter to cover pan with a very thin layer. When cooked on one side, toss or turn with a spatula and cook other side. Wrap in foil and store in refrigerator overnight, if desired. Blend 2 tablespoons flour with minced steak. Melt butter in saucepan, add onion, garlic, salt and pepper and toss over heat until it browns. Add tomato purée gradually, stirring constantly until it boils. Reduce heat, simmer 30 minutes. The mixture must be very thick. If too thin, remove from heat and sprinkle over 1 tablespoon flour. Return to heat and cook, stirring, 1 minute. Allow to cool. Roll a portion of meat into each pancake, folding in ends neatly. Place side by side in shallow ovenproof dish. Pour over Cheese Sauce, cover with greased paper and bake in moderately hot oven for 30 minutes. Garnish with parsley.

CHEESE SAUCE: Melt butter in saucepan, stir in flour and gradually add warm milk. Stir constantly until sauce is thick and creamy. Season with salt and pepper to taste. Add cheese, heat but do not boil. Allow to cool.

Beef Casserole Continental

(Serves 4-6)
1½ lb. topside steak
seasoned flour
1 oz. clarified butter
1 tablespoon plain flour
1 cup water
1 lb. ripe tomatoes
2 large onions
1 cup diced carrots
2 bayleaves
salt, pepper
2 teaspoons sugar
2 teaspoons worcestershire sauce

CHEESE AND RICE TOPPING
3 cups cooked rice
1 cup grated matured cheese
1 egg
½ teaspoon dry mustard
salt, pepper

Trim meat, cut into 1-in. squares. Coat in flour seasoned with salt and pepper. Melt butter in pan, fry meat until lightly browned; remove from pan, set aside. Work the 1 tablespoon flour into butter left in the pan, blending with the back of spoon until smooth and brown; gradually add water and stir until gravy thickens. Add meat, skinned and diced tomatoes, sliced onions, carrots, and bayleaves. Season with salt, pepper, sugar and sauce; mix well. Cover, cook gently until meat is tender (about 50 to 60 minutes). Drain boiled rice and, while still warm, stir in beaten egg, cheese, mustard, salt and pepper. Just before serving, pour the cooked beef into a greased shallow ovenproof dish. Arrange the hot rice and cheese mixture round edge of dish. Place dish under griller at moderate heat, cook until browned lightly.

Lamb Chops in a Crust

4 thick lamb loin or rib chops
salt and pepper
4 oz. mushrooms, sliced and sautéed in 2 oz. butter
1 clove garlic
1 egg lightly beaten

CRUST
1¼ cups plain flour
salt and pepper
3 oz. butter
1 egg-yolk
2 tablespoons iced water

Remove bone from chops. Sprinkle with salt and pepper and grill 2 minutes each side. Cool. Chop mushrooms and garlic finely, spread both sides of chops with a thin coating of the mixture and enclose each in a pastry square. Seal edges by moistening with water and pressing with fingers. Brush tops with egg. Bake in moderately hot oven for 30 minutes.

CRUST: Sift flour with salt and pepper. Cut in butter. Quickly blend in egg-yolk with fingertips. Stir in water a little at a time to make a firm dough. Chill. Roll out thinly and cut into squares large enough to enclose a prepared chop.

Prawns Ballina

(Serves 6-8)
6 oz. butter
2 lb. uncooked prawns, shelled and deveined
1 dessertspoon flour
8 oz. thinly sliced mushrooms
8 oz. sour cream
freshly ground black pepper
1 cup finely chopped shallots, including green tops
salt

Melt 4 oz. butter in pan, add the shallots and prawns. Cook, stirring, turning the prawns until they just turn pink (3 to 5 minutes). Do not overcook. Sprinkle with salt and pepper to taste and set aside. Melt remaining butter in another pan, and cook the mushrooms until they give up their liquid. Continue cooking until most of this liquid has evaporated. Stir in the flour, add salt and pepper to taste; add prawn mixture and carefully stir in the sour cream. Heat thoroughly but do not boil or the cream may curdle. Serve hot with rice.

Stuffed Chicken Breasts with Orange Salad

(Serves 6)
6 large chicken breasts, boned
2 tablespoons plain flour
1 teaspoon paprika
½ teaspoon garlic salt
juice 1 large orange
1 small onion finely chopped
2 oz. butter
½ pint chicken stock
salt and pepper to taste
2 in. stick cinnamon
1 teaspoon cornflour
6 orange slices
little cold water

STUFFING
¾ cup seedless raisins
2 tablespoons sherry
1 oz. butter
¼ cup finely diced ham
1 tablespoon parsley
grated rind ½ orange
½ cup soft white breadcrumbs

ORANGE SALAD
1 tablespoon seedless raisins
2 medium-sized oranges
½ medium-sized cucumber
½ cup chopped walnuts
4 sticks celery
good squeeze lemon juice
1 medium-sized lettuce
salt and pepper to taste

Soak raisins in sherry for about ½ hour. Chop half the raisins (leaving remainder for sauce), add softened butter, ham, parsley, orange rind and breadcrumbs; mix well. Lay chicken breasts on board, skin side down. Divide stuffing into six equal portions and place a portion on centre of each chicken breast. Fold over chicken to enclose stuffing and secure with small wooden sticks. Mix flour, paprika, and garlic salt and use to coat each breast thoroughly. Fry breasts in hot butter, turning to brown all sides. Drain off excess butter, pour orange juice and stock over chicken. Add onion, seasoning and cinnamon. Cover and simmer gently until chicken is tender (about 30 to 40 minutes). Remove cinnamon stick, add remaining raisins. Mix cornflour with a little cold water, stir into sauce, simmer further 3 to 4 minutes stirring frequently. Remove sticks. Place each chicken breast on orange slice. Pour sauce over. Serve with Orange Salad.

ORANGE SALAD: Put the raisins into boiling water for 1 to 2 minutes to soften, then drain well. Peel oranges, remove all white pith, cut into sections. Cut cucumber into small strips, slice celery finely. Place lettuce, torn into pieces, into serving bowl, add celery and half the cucumber strips, toss lightly. Add the raisins, sprinkle with lemon juice, salt and pepper. Add orange sections, chopped walnuts and top with remaining cucumber strips.

Chickacheese Pie

¾ cup sliced celery
4 oz. can mushrooms
⅓ cup chopped onion
2 oz. butter
1 tablespoon plain flour
1 cup chicken broth
salt, pepper
1½ cups cubed and cooked chicken
3 eggs, separated
1⅓ cups sour cream
1 cup (4 oz.) self-raising flour
1½ cups shredded cheddar cheese

CHEESE SAUCE
2 oz. butter
3 tablespoons plain flour
1½ cups milk
½ cup cream
1 cup grated cheddar cheese
1 tablespoon grated parmesan cheese
¼ teaspoon onion juice
⅛ teaspoon curry powder

Cook celery and onion in butter until just tender. Stir in plain flour and pinch salt. Cook 1 minute. Add chicken broth and canned mushrooms, cook over low heat, stirring constantly until mixture thickens and boils. Add a dash of pepper and cooked chicken. Set aside. Blend together egg-yolks and sour cream in a large bowl. Stir in self-raising flour and ½ teaspoon salt. Beat egg-whites until stiff, but not dry, and fold into egg-yolk mixture gently but thoroughly. Pour half egg mixture into a well greased 9-in. pie plate or shallow casserole. Top with ½ cup cheese. Bake in a moderate oven (350°G, 375°E) 10 minutes. Remove from oven. Place chicken mixture on top, pour remaining batter over chicken. Bake 15 minutes longer until light golden brown. Top with remaining 1 cup cheese and return to oven 1 minute until cheese melts slightly. Serve hot with Cheese Sauce.

CHEESE SAUCE: Melt butter, blend in flour. Add milk and cream and stir until thickened. Add cheese, onion juice and curry powder. Continue heating and stirring until cheese melts and flavours are blended.

Stuffed Chicken Breasts with Orange Salad

Tournedos Australian

(Serves 4)
1 fresh ripe pineapple
plain flour
2 oz. butter
8 slices bread
freshly ground pepper
clarified butter
8 tournedos (thick slices fillet steak)
3 teaspoons grated macadamia nuts

PINEAPPLE BUTTER SAUCE
½ cup canned pineapple juice
1 tablespoon finely chopped onion
1 tablespoon vinegar
salt, cayenne
1 teaspoon tarragon leaves
2 egg-yolks
4 oz. butter, melted
1 teaspoon finely chopped parsley

Peel pineapple, slice into eight ½-in. thick rounds; remove core. Place pineapple under griller until dry on the surface. Dust lightly with plain flour. Dot each round with butter and replace under the griller until beginning to brown slightly; keep hot. Cut bread into rounds the same size as the pineapple. Fry in clarified butter until crisp; turn once. Keep hot. Season tournedos with freshly ground black pepper; dust lightly with little plain flour. Fry in clarified butter until cooked as desired. Place a round of pineapple on each round of bread, top with a tournedos. Spoon Pineapple Butter Sauce on top of each tournedos and sprinkle with grated macadamia nuts.

PINEAPPLE BUTTER SAUCE: Combine pineapple juice, onion, vinegar and tarragon in small saucepan. Bring to the boil; simmer 10 minutes, until reduced to ⅓ cup. Strain. Off heat in top of double boiler, beat egg-yolks lightly, stir in half the melted butter; cook, beating continually, over simmering water until warmed through. Add strained liquid alternately with remaining melted butter; continue beating until sauce is thick and fluffy. Remove from heat at once, stir in seasonings and parsley. Serve immediately.

Hazelnut Rum Cake

8 oz. butter
1 cup castor sugar
4 eggs, separated
grated rind ½ lemon
4 oz. ground hazelnuts
2 tablespoons rum
2 cups self-raising flour

DECORATION
3 oz. dark chocolate, melted
few whole hazelnuts

Cream butter and sugar; add egg-yolks one at a time, beating well after each addition. Add lemon rind, ground hazelnuts and rum. Fold in sifted flour. Beat egg-whites until stiff, fold into flour mixture. Pour into greased 8-in. baba tin; bake in moderate oven approximately 1 hour, or until cooked when tested; cool.

DECORATION: When cold, pour melted chocolate over the top and allow to trickle unevenly down sides. Decorate with hazelnuts.

Ginger Cream Cake

3 oz. butter
½ cup castor sugar
2 eggs, separated
1½ cups self-raising flour
pinch salt
¼ cup milk
1 tablespoon ginger syrup
1 teaspoon vanilla
1 tablespoon finely chopped preserved ginger

FROSTING
4 oz. cream cheese
2 cups icing sugar
1 teaspoon ginger syrup
1 teaspoon milk
2 tablespoons finely chopped preserved ginger

Butter and line a round 7-in. cake tin. Cream butter and sugar together until light and fluffy, then add egg-yolks and beat well. Fold in sifted flour and salt alternately with milk, ginger syrup and vanilla. Add preserved ginger, then fold in stiffly beaten egg-whites. Spoon into cake tin. Bake in moderately hot oven 50 to 55 minutes. When cooked, turn on to cake cooler. When completely cool, cover with frosting.

FROSTING: Soften cream cheese in warm basin, then cream it with milk and syrup, gradually work in sifted icing sugar and chopped ginger. Spread thickly over cake and swirl with a fork.

Royal Chocolate Cake

2 cups self-raising flour
½ cup cocoa
4 oz. butter
1½ cups sugar
3 unbeaten egg-whites
¾ cup water
¾ cup sour cream
1 teaspoon vanilla

DECORATION
glacé orange slices, halved or orange segment jubes
angelica

ORANGE CREAM
2 oz. butter
2 tablespoons icing sugar
2 tablespoons condensed milk
2 tablespoons orange juice
½ teaspoon grated orange rind
extra icing sugar if necessary

SOFT BITTERSWEET FROSTING
4 oz. cooking chocolate
3 tablespoons hot water
1½ cups icing sugar
1 egg
2 oz. butter
1 teaspoon vanilla

Cream butter, gradually add sugar, creaming well. Add unbeaten egg-whites, beat one minute. Combine water, sour cream and vanilla. Add alternately to the creamed mixture with the sifted dry ingredients. Blend well after each addition. Pour into two 8-in. round sandwich tins, well-greased and lightly-floured. Bake in moderate oven 25 to 30 minutes. Cool and join together with Orange Cream, frost with frosting, decorate.

ORANGE CREAM: Beat butter until soft, gradually add sifted icing sugar, condensed milk, orange juice and rind. Whip with rotary beater until consistency of whipped cream.

SOFT BITTERSWEET FROSTING: Melt chopped chocolate over low heat. Add hot water, stir until thick and smooth. Remove from heat, blend in sifted icing sugar; add egg and beat until smooth. Add softened butter a little at a time, beating after each addition; add vanilla.

Hazelnut Rum Cak

Golden Coffee Cake

4 oz. butter
1 cup brown sugar, firmly packed
½ teaspoon vanilla
2 eggs, separated
2 tablespoons golden syrup
½ cup chopped walnuts
2 cups self-raising flour
1 teaspoon cinnamon
½ teaspoon nutmeg
½ teaspoon ground cloves
¼ teaspoon salt
½ cup milk

FROSTING

1 oz. butter
4 tablespoons icing sugar
1 teaspoon cocoa
1 dessertspoon milk
1 teaspoon coffee essence
3 tablespoons full cream milk powder
walnut halves to decorate

Cream butter with sugar and vanilla, add egg-yolks one at a time, beating well after each addition. Add golden syrup and walnuts. Fold in flour, sifted with spices and salt, alternately with milk. Fold in stiffly beaten egg-whites. Turn into buttered 7-in. or 8-in. cake tin, bake in moderate oven 1 to 1½ hours. Stand in tin a few minutes before turning on to cake cooler. When cold, frost and decorate with walnut halves.

FROSTING: Beat butter until soft, gradually add icing sugar. Beat in half the milk, the coffee essence and cocoa. Gradually beat in powdered milk, remaining fresh milk and continue beating until smooth. Spread over top of cake, rough up with fork, decorate with walnut halves.

Sunshine State Cake

1 cup peanuts
½ cup brown sugar
2 oz. melted butter
4 oz. butter
½ cup sugar
2 eggs
2 cups self-raising flour
2 oz. chopped peanuts
2 oz. chopped crystallized ginger
½ cup milk
1 teaspoon vanilla

Butter a loaf tin (9 in. x 5 in.) and line base with greaseproof paper. Sprinkle with peanuts and brown sugar. Pour over 2 oz. melted butter, allow to set firm. Cream butter with sugar, add eggs and beat well. Fold in sifted flour alternately with milk, add vanilla. Mix in ginger and chopped peanuts. Pour into tin over peanut base and bake in moderate oven 50 to 60 minutes. Leave in tin a few minutes before turning out to cool.

Festival Ribbon Cake

4 oz. butter
6 oz. light brown sugar
2 teaspoons unsweetened coffee essence
1 teaspoon rum
3 eggs
8 oz. self-raising flour
4 oz. milk
1 tablespoon cocoa
1 dessertspoon milk

FILLING

6 oz. butter
6 oz. pure icing sugar
2 tablespoons coffee essence
2 teaspoons rum

TOFFEE

6 oz. white sugar
1 teaspoon butter
4 tablespoons water

Cream together butter and brown sugar then beat in coffee essence and rum. Whisk eggs and add gradually to the butter/sugar mixture. Fold in flour alternately with milk. Place half the mixture in one 8-in. sandwich pan—then to the other half add cocoa blended with one dessertspoon milk. Fold through mixture evenly and place in another 8-in. sandwich pan. Bake at 350°-375° moderate oven for 35-40 minutes. Cool thoroughly.

FILLING: Cream together butter, icing sugar, coffee essence and rum.

TOFFEE: Blend sugar, butter and water together in a small saucepan and cook over a low heat until golden brown and it 'cracks' when dropped into cold water.

TO ASSEMBLE: Carefully split each layer in half, stack light and dark layers alternately spreading each layer with rum coffee cream. Leave top uncreamed. Fasten a stiff band of brown paper around side of cake making sure it extends above the top of the cake. When toffee is at the 'crack' stage, quickly pour over top of cake taking care it does not run down the protected sides. To make it easier for cutting, mark the surface with the back of a long knife into 10 slices. Remove paper when toffee is set. Finally cream sides of cake and decorate with 1 oz. walnut pieces and 2 oz. finely chopped walnuts.

Caramel Sauce Cake

2 cups brown sugar (firmly packed)
¼ cup butter
2 tablespoons water
¼ teaspoon salt
1 cup evaporated milk
2 teaspoons vanilla
2¼ cups plain flour
1 teaspoon baking powder
1 teaspoon bicarbonate of soda
1 teaspoon salt
½ cup soft butter
½ cup milk
3 eggs

CREAMY CARAMEL FROSTING
3 oz. softened cream cheese
3 cups sifted icing sugar
1 teaspoon vanilla
pecan or walnut halves

Combine brown sugar, ¼ cup butter and water and salt in saucepan. Cook over medium heat stirring constantly until little syrup dropped in cold water forms a soft ball. Remove from heat. Add evaporated milk and vanilla. Cool thoroughly. Sift together flour, baking powder, soda and salt into a large bowl. Add ½ cup soft butter, ½ cup milk and 2 cups of the caramel sauce. (Reserve remaining sauce). Beat on low speed about 1½ minutes. Add unbeaten eggs and beat a further 1½ minutes. Bake in two well-greased and lightly-floured tins (approximately 9 in.) for 35 to 40 minutes at 350°. When cool join together and frost with Creamy Caramel Frosting.

CREAMY CARAMEL FROSTING: Cream the remaining caramel sauce with softened cream cheese. Gradually blend in sifted icing sugar. Beat until smooth and of spreading consistency. Add vanilla. If necessary thin with a little milk or cream. Decorate with pecan or walnut halves.

Chocolate Macaroon Cake

4 oz. butter
¾ cup sugar
2 egg-yolks
3 tablespoons coconut
2 cups self-raising flour
3 dessertspoons cocoa
1 cup milk
pinch salt
raspberry jam

TOPPING
2 egg-whites
½ cup sugar
½ cup coconut
pinch salt

Cream butter and sugar. Add egg-yolks and coconut. Mix well. Add flour and cocoa, alternately with milk. Put into a greased and floured slab tin 7 in. x 10 in. Spread with a thin layer of raspberry jam.

TOPPING: Beat egg-whites and salt until stiff. Gradually add sugar and beat well. Fold in coconut and spread over cake. Bake in moderate oven (375°F.) for 30 to 35 minutes.

Golden Fruits Festive Cake

4 oz. crystallized or glacé cumquats
4 oz. glacé apricots or pineapple
2 oz. almonds, blanched, split and browned
6 oz. butter
¾ cup castor sugar
1 teaspoon grated lemon rind
1 teaspoon grated orange rind
3 eggs
2 cups plain flour
½ cup self-raising flour
¼ teaspoon salt
2 tablespoons milk or sherry

Line a 7-in. round cake tin with 2 layers of buttered, brown paper. Cut fruits with kitchen scissors and prepare almonds. Cream butter and sugar with lemon and orange rinds. Add eggs one at a time. Mix in fruits and sifted flours and salt alternately. Lastly blend in milk or sherry. Turn into prepared tin and bake 1 to 1¼ hours in moderate oven.

Nougat Cake

2 cups self-raising flour
¼ teaspoon salt
1 teaspoon bicarbonate of soda
2 oz. cooking chocolate, grated
1 tablespoon honey
½ cup milk
1½ cups sifted icing sugar
4 oz. butter
2 eggs
1 teaspoon vanilla
whipped cream
icing sugar to decorate

Sift flour, salt and bicarbonate of soda. Melt chocolate over hot water, add honey, ¼ cup milk and ¼ cup icing sugar, stir until smooth. Cool slightly. Cream butter with remaining icing sugar. Add eggs one at a time and beat well. Add vanilla to remaining milk and fold into creamed mixture alternately with dry ingredients. Lastly add chocolate-honey mixture. Pour into 2 well buttered 8-in. sandwich tins and bake in moderate oven 25 minutes or until done. Cool, fill with cream and dust top with icing sugar.

Orange Ripple Buttercake

2 oz. dark cooking chocolate
4 oz. soft butter
8 oz. sugar
3 eggs
grated rind of 1 orange
½ cup orange juice
¼ cup milk
10 oz. (2½ cups) self-raising flour

ORANGE BUTTER FROSTING
1 tablespoon soft butter
8 oz. (1½ cups) sifted icing sugar
2-3 tablespoons orange juice

Grate chocolate. Cream butter and sugar till light and fluffy. Add eggs one at a time, beating well after each. Mix in orange rind and juice. Fold in milk and sifted flour. Butter a deep 8-in. cake tin. Spread a thin layer of cake batter on the bottom. Sprinkle with some of the grated chocolate. Spoon in remaining batter, sprinkling each addition with chocolate. Bake in a moderate oven (350°) for about 1 hour. When cold cover with Orange Butter Frosting.

ORANGE BUTTER FROSTING: Cream the butter, add the icing sugar, then beat to a spreading consistency with the orange juice.

Chocolate Macaroon Cake

Cherry Yoghurt Cake

4 oz. butter
1 cup castor sugar
grated rind 1 lemon
3 eggs, separated
1½ cups self-raising flour
¼ cup yoghurt
2 oz. chopped glacé cherries
lemon icing
extra large cherries to decorate

Cream butter and castor sugar, add lemon rind and beat well. Add egg-yolks one at a time beating well. Fold in sifted flour alternately with yoghurt. Stir in chopped cherries. Beat egg-whites until stiff, fold into batter. Spoon into a buttered loaf tin. Bake in moderate oven 1 hour. Cool. Ice with lemon icing and decorate with cherries.

Almond Butter Cream Cake

4 oz. butter
¾ cup sugar
2 eggs
2 oz. cornflour
juice of ½ lemon
2 cups self-raising flour
glacé cherries

FILLING
⅓ cup sugar
2 oz. custard powder
1 pint milk
8 oz. unsalted butter

ROASTED ALMONDS
6 oz. blanched almonds, chopped
1 tablespoon sugar
little butter

Cream butter, add sugar, eggs, and beat until smooth. Mix in cornflour, lemon juice and flour. Bake in a buttered 8-in. ring cake tin in moderate oven 45 to 50 minutes. Cool and cut into 3 layers. Spread and cover with filling, reserving some for decoration. Decorate with roasted almonds, reserved filling and cherries.

FILLING: Blend sugar and custard powder with a little cold milk. Heat remaining milk and pour on to custard mixture, stirring constantly. Return to saucepan and cook stirring, until thick. Stand saucepan in cold water and stir constantly until cool. Cream butter, gradually add custard, beating until smooth after each addition.

ROASTED ALMONDS: Melt butter in frying pan, add sugar and chopped almonds. Stir until light brown. Cool.

Gold Coast Layer Cake

2¼ cups self-raising flour
1 cup sugar
1 teaspoon salt
1 teaspoon cinnamon
1 teaspoon nutmeg
½ teaspoon ground cloves
½ teaspoon allspice
¾ cup packed brown sugar
½ cup soft butter
1 cup skim milk
3 eggs

CHOCOLATE BUTTER CREAM
6 oz. butter
4 oz. icing sugar
1 egg-yolk
2 oz. dark block chocolate
2 tablespoons cocoa
little milk

TOFFEE
⅔ cup sugar
¼ teaspoon cream of tartar
⅓ cup water

DECORATION
chopped walnuts
shredded coconut or chocolate sprinkles

Sift flour, sugar, salt, cinnamon, nutmeg, ground cloves and allspice into a bowl. Add brown sugar, soft butter and skim milk. Beat 2 minutes on medium speed on electric mixer or 300 vigorous strokes by hand. Scrape sides and bottom of bowl constantly. Add eggs and beat 2 minutes longer, scraping bowl frequently. Pour into two 9-in. layer tins which have been well-greased and floured. Bake at 350° for 35-40 minutes or until cake springs back when lightly pressed in the centre. Cool. Cut each cake through the centre (4 layers). Spread each slice with a generous layer of butter cream. Reserve enough to coat the sides, fasten band of tight brown paper around cake. Pour toffee over. Smooth toffee with a wet knife then with a well-greased knife mark indentations in the unset toffee, cutting into 10 sections. Remove paper. Coat the sides of cake with the remaining butter cream. Press chopped walnuts, shredded coconut or chocolate sprinkles around sides. If liked, decorate top with almond halves in a flower petal design.

CHOCOLATE BUTTER CREAM: Cream butter until fluffy, add icing sugar, then egg-yolk very gradually. Melt block chocolate on a saucer over hot water. Mix well, cool. Mix cocoa to a firm paste with a little milk and add to the butter mixture. When chocolate is cool mix well to eliminate lumps and add to the butter cream.

TOFFEE: Dissolve sugar and cream of tartar in water. Stir until boiling. Do not stir after it has boiled. Cook until a golden brown colour.

Sherried Almond Date Cake

DATE MIXTURE
10 oz. chopped dates
grated rind of 1 large orange
3 tablespoons orange juice
2 tablespoons sweet sherry
1 teaspoon cinnamon
½ teaspoon ground ginger

ALMOND CAKE
6 oz. butter
6 oz. castor sugar
3 egg-yolks
1 oz. almond meal
2 dessertspoons sweet orange marmalade
2 tablespoons sweet sherry
1 teaspoon almond essence
7 oz. self-raising flour (sift twice)
2 oz. plain flour (sift twice)
3 well-beaten egg-whites

ICING
6 oz. icing sugar
reserved date mixture
1 teaspoon soft butter
1 tablespoon water

DATE MIXTURE: Place all ingredients into a saucepan and cook over a low heat until soft and well blended. Take out 1 tablespoon and place in a basin, put aside to be used in the icing. Allow the rest of the date mixture to become quite cold.

CAKE: Cream butter and sugar, add egg-yolks one at a time and beat well. Add almond meal, marmalade, sweet sherry and almond essence mixing well after each addition. Fold in $^3/_4$ of the sifted flour, then add the well-beaten egg-whites, lastly fold in the remaining flour. Next distribute teaspoons of the date mixture into the cake batter then lightly mix through. Place in a well-greased and papered 7-in. square tin and bake at 375° for 1 hour. Leave for a few minutes, then carefully turn out. When cold cover top with icing.

ICING: Combine all ingredients and mix well.

Apple Currant Cakelets

4 oz. butter
6 oz. brown sugar
1 teaspoon lemon juice
2 eggs
8 oz. self-raising flour
1 teaspoon cinnamon
½ teaspoon nutmeg
¼ teaspoon salt
¾ cup milk
¾ cup currants
1 tablespoon chopped mixed peel

APPLE FILLING
3 large cooking apples
4 oz. sugar
2 tablespoons water
1 teaspoon butter
1 teaspoon lemon juice
1 teaspoon cinnamon

Cream butter and sugar with lemon juice until a smooth cream, add eggs one at a time beating well after each addition, then add sifted dry ingredients alternately with milk, lastly add currants and peel. Place spoonful in each well-greased patty tin, hollowing centre to form a nest with base and sides covered, then put teaspoonful of hot apple mixture in each. Cover with a little more cake mixture (if stiff add a little more milk). Bake in moderate oven 350°G about 10 minutes. Serve hot or cold, dusted with icing sugar.

APPLE FILLING: Cook peeled, sliced apples in water with sugar gently until soft, mash with other ingredients into a smooth pulp.

Spanish Lemon Cake

4 oz. butter
4 oz. sugar
3 oz. brown sugar
2 eggs
2 cups (8 oz.) plain flour
2 teaspoons bicarbonate of soda
1 lemon, medium sized
1 cup dates
1 cup sour cream

FROSTING
3 tablespoons butter
1½ cups pure icing sugar
3 tablespoons sour cream
pinch salt
½ teaspoon vanilla essence
1 teaspoon lemon juice

Cream together butter and sugars until light. Add gradually lightly-beaten eggs, beating well after each addition. Sift once flour and bi-carbonate of soda. Cut lemon in halves and carefully remove all seeds. Chop up finely, or grind in a food blender together with dates, place in a mixing bowl, add ½ cup flour mixture to this and mix together lightly with a fork. Fold in dry ingredients and fruit mixture alternately with sour cream. Place mixture in two 8-in. well-greased and floured sandwich pans and bake in a moderate oven (350°) for 35 minutes. Cool thoroughly. Sandwich cakes together with cream frosting then use remaining frosting to cover top and sides, decorate with coarse lemon-tinted coconut.

FROSTING: Cream butter until soft, add icing sugar gradually, add sour cream, salt, vanilla essence and lemon juice beating all together well.

Apple Cake Deluxe

2 cups sweetened apple pulp
4 oz. butter
1 cup castor sugar
1 egg
2 tablespoons cocoa
1 cup milk
1 teaspoon bicarbonate of soda
2 cups (8 oz.) self-raising flour
pinch salt
2 egg-whites (reserve yolks for the lemon butter)
4 tablespoons sugar

LEMON BUTTER
grated rind and juice 2 lemons
2 oz. butter
4 oz. sugar
2 egg-yolks

Place apple pulp in the base of a buttered ovenproof dish. Cream butter and sugar until light and fluffy. Add egg and beat well. Blend cocoa smoothly with milk, then add bicarbonate of soda. Fold sifted flour and salt alternately with milk into creamed mixture. Spread smoothly over top of apple. Place in a moderate oven (350°G, 375°E) and bake 50-60 minutes or until cooked through. Remove from oven and allow to cool slightly. Beat egg-whites until stiff, gradually add sugar and beat until sugar dissolves. Spoon in rough dobs on top of dessert. Return to moderate oven until meringue browns slightly. Remove from oven, spoon over lemon butter.

LEMON BUTTER: Place lemon rind, juice, butter, sugar and egg-yolks in a saucepan and stir over low heat until well mixed and thickened slightly. Cool before serving.

Apple Currant Cakelet

Ginger-Lemon Butter Cake

LEMON BUTTER
4 oz. butter
½ cup sugar
4 egg-yolks
3 tablespoons lemon juice

GINGER CAKE
4 oz. butter
⅓ cup castor sugar
2 eggs
2 cups self-raising flour
1 teaspoon ground ginger
½ teaspoon mixed spice
1 tablespoon golden syrup and enough milk to make ½ cup liquid
3 oz. finely chopped crystallized ginger
extra ginger

SPICY ICING
1½ oz. butter
¼ teaspoon cinnamon
1 teaspoon golden syrup
4-5 drops lemon essence
1½ cups sifted icing sugar

LEMON BUTTER: Put butter, sugar, egg-yolks and lemon juice in top of double saucepan and cook gently, stirring constantly until mixture thickens (15 minutes). Cool thoroughly. Lemon Butter may be made the day before.

GINGER CAKE: Cream together butter and sugar. Add beaten eggs, a little at a time. Sift flour and spices together twice and fold into creamed mixture alternately with golden syrup and milk. Add chopped ginger which has been lightly tossed in flour. Put into a buttered 7-in. cake tin working it up a little around sides. Spread with cold Lemon Butter, then spoon in remaining cake mixture. Bake in moderate oven 1 hour. Leave 5 minutes and remove cake from pan. When cold, top with Spicy Icing and small pieces of ginger.

SPICY ICING: Cream butter. Add cinnamon, golden syrup, lemon essence, icing sugar and a little warm water to mix. Beat well.

Cider Butter Cake

4 oz. butter
½ cup castor sugar
2 eggs
2 cups plain flour
½ teaspoon ground ginger
pinch nutmeg
½ teaspoon bicarbonate of soda
pinch salt
¼ pint apple cider
chopped toasted peanuts to decorate

CREAM CHEESE LEMON ICING
2 oz. cream cheese
1 tablespoon lemon juice
4 oz. icing sugar
cream or evaporated milk

Cream butter and sugar until light and fluffy. Add eggs, blend well. Sift flour, ginger, nutmeg, bicarbonate of soda and salt, add half to creamed mixture. Whisk cider until frothy and add. Stir in remaining flour and blend until smooth. Turn mixture into buttered and lined shallow tin (approximately 11 in. x 7 in. x 1½ in.). Bake in moderate oven 35 minutes. Cool. Spread with Cream Cheese Lemon Icing, decorate with peanuts.

CREAM CHEESE LEMON ICING: Soften cheese with lemon juice and beat until smooth. Blend in icing sugar and a little cream or milk if needed to give a good spreading consistency.

Upside-down-cake

1½ oz. butter, melted
3 tablespoons brown sugar
¾ cup dried apricots or peaches or a mixture of both, soaked in water to cover about 3 hours
½ cup prunes
¼ cup blanched almonds
3 oz. butter
¾ cup sugar
2 eggs
1½ cups self-raising flour
pinch salt
¼ cup milk

Combine melted butter and brown sugar. Press into well-buttered 8-in. square cake tin. Arrange dried fruits and blanched almonds in pattern on butter and sugar mixture. Cream butter and sugar until light. Add eggs, one at a time, beating well after each. Sift flour and salt and fold into mixture alternately with milk. Pour into prepared tin and bake in moderate oven about 40 minutes or until cooked when fine skewer inserted will come out clean. Cool in tin on wire rack 5 minutes. Turn out on to serving plate and serve warm.

Berry Kuchen

2 oz. crushed wheatflakes
6 oz. berry jam
4 eggs
pinch salt
8 oz. sugar
8 oz. plain flour
1 tablespoon rum
1 tablespoon lemon juice
8 oz. butter
1 teaspoon baking powder
1½ tablespoons flour

TOPPING
2 oz. cream cheese
3 oz. sifted icing sugar
1 teaspoon lemon juice
2 tablespoons chopped walnuts

Set oven at 400° or to moderate. Line 8-in. round tin with 2 layers of greaseproof paper. Combine wheatflakes and jam and set aside. Separate whites from yolks of eggs. Beat whites with pinch of salt until stiff. Gradually add sugar and beat until well combined. Beat in yolks one by one. Slowly fold in twice sifted flour with a knife and then add rum and lemon juice. Add boiling, foaming butter, then the teaspoon baking powder mixed with the extra flour. Quickly mix and pour ¾ of mixture into lined tin. Spread jam mixture over this layer and then add remainder of flour mixture. Bake in middle of a moderate oven for 50-60 minutes.

TOPPING: Beat cream cheese until soft. Gradually add icing sugar. Add lemon juice. Spread over top of cool cake. Sprinkle with walnuts.

Chocolate Delight Cake

2½ cups self-raising flour
6 oz. butter
1 cup sugar
1 tablespoon golden syrup
½ teaspoon carbonate of soda
½ cup hot water
½ cup milk
2 eggs
½ teaspoon vanilla
2 tablespoons dark cocoa
½ teaspoon each spice, salt, nutmeg, ground cloves

FILLING
2 tablespoons poppy seeds
3 tablespoons cream
3 tablespoons clear honey
4 oz. butter
3 tablespoons icing sugar
2 tablespoons grated chocolate
¼ teaspoon each spice, nutmeg
½ teaspoon vanilla
8 oz. cooking chocolate

Place sugar, syrup, butter, cocoa, soda in a bowl. Pour hot water over it. Stir for 1 minute. Add sifted flour, salt and spices. Place on low speed and mix for 1 minute. Drop in the eggs. Add the milk. Place on medium speed for 4 minutes. Turn up to a slightly higher speed for 2 minutes more. Turn into buttered 8-in. sandwich pans. Bake for 27 minutes at 375°. Cool. Fill with half the filling and place remainder on top and sides. Melt cooking chocolate over hot water. Carefully cover the complete cake with chocolate. Decorate with chocolate roses and leaves. Sprinkle the leaves with poppy seeds.

FILLING: Place poppy seeds in cream and add the honey. Cook gently 7 minutes then remove from heat and cool. Cream butter, icing sugar and chocolate, add spices. Gradually add the cream mixture to the creamed butter. Add vanilla.

Apple and Nut Family Cake

3 cups plain flour
6 oz. butter
¾ cup castor sugar
1 teaspoon cinnamon
½ pint apple puree
12 oz. chopped dates and nuts (combined)
1½ teaspoons bicarbonate of soda
2-3 tablespoons milk

TOPPING
1 tablespoon chopped dates and nuts
2 dessertspoons sugar
1 teaspoon cinnamon

Butter and line 8-in. round cake tin. Sift flour, rub in the butter until the mixture resembles fine breadcrumbs. Add sugar, cinnamon, dates and nuts. Make a well in the centre, add the apple purée. Dissolve bicarbonate of soda in milk and add to mixture, mixing well. Put into tin, sprinkle with combined topping ingredients. Bake in a moderate oven 1¼ to 1½ hours.

Chocolate-Cheese Fudge Cake

4 oz. butter
4 oz. processed cream cheese
1 cup castor sugar
1 cup brown sugar
2 eggs
1 cup chopped walnuts
2⅔ cups (10½ oz.) self-raising flour
¼ cup cocoa
¼ teaspoon bicarbonate of soda
¼ teaspoon salt
1 cup sour milk

FROSTING
½ cup cream or evaporated milk
2 oz. butter
3½ cups sifted icing sugar
¼ teaspoon salt
3 oz. dark chocolate
1 teaspoon vanilla
whipped cream

Cream butter and cream cheese with sugars until light and fluffy. Add eggs one at a time, beating well after each addition. Stir in walnuts. Fold in sifted flour, cocoa, bicarbonate of soda and salt alternately with sour milk. Fill into well-greased and lightly-floured 8-in. sandwich tins. Bake in a moderate oven (350°G, 375°E) 40-45 minutes. Turn out on cake cooler. Allow to cool. Sandwich cake with stiffly whipped cream and cover with frosting.

FROSTING: Heat cream with butter until butter has melted. Remove from heat. Gradually add sifted icing sugar and salt. Add melted chocolate and vanilla. Beat all together over ice until thickened to spreading consistency.

Chocolate Delight Cake

Cheese Cocoa Cake

4 oz. butter
2 4-oz. packets cream cheese
1 cup sugar
1 cup firmly packed brown sugar
2 eggs
1 cup chopped walnuts
2⅔ cups plain flour
¼ cup cocoa
1 teaspoon bicarbonate of soda
1 teaspoon baking powder
1 teaspoon salt
1¼ cups sour milk

SPEEDY FUDGE FROSTING
½ cup cream or evaporated milk
2 oz. butter
3 cups sifted icing sugar
¼ teaspoon salt
1 teaspoon vanilla
3 oz. chocolate, melted

Cream butter and cream cheese with both kinds of sugar until light and fluffy. Add unbeaten eggs one at a time, beating well after each addition, then stir in walnuts. Fold in sifted dry ingredients alternately with sour milk. Put into well-buttered and lightly-floured large slab tin (12 in. x 9 in. x 2½ in.) and bake in moderate oven 45 to 50 minutes. Turn out to cool on wire rack. When cool, cover with frosting.

SPEEDY FUDGE FROSTING: Heat cream or evaporated milk with butter until butter is melted. Remove from heat, gradually add icing sugar and salt. Lastly add vanilla and melted chocolate and beat until thickened to spreading consistency.

Crunchy Amber Cake

4 oz. butter
1 cup brown sugar
1 whole egg
1 egg-yolk
1 teaspoon vanilla
1½ cups self-raising flour
½ cup milk

FILLING
3 oz. butter
4 tablespoons brown sugar
2 tablespoons cornflour
pinch salt
1 egg-yolk
1 cup milk
½ teaspoon vanilla

TOPPING
2 egg-whites
½ cup sugar
1 tablespoon coconut
1 tablespoon sugar
1 teaspoon cinnamon
1 tablespoon slivered almonds

Cream butter and sugar until light and fluffy. Add egg, egg-yolk and vanilla and beat lightly. Fold in sifted flour alternately with milk, stirring well. Divide mixture evenly in 2 buttered and floured round 8-in. tins. Bake in moderate oven 20 minutes. Turn out to cool. Sandwich cakes with filling. Spread topping on cake and sprinkle with combined coconut, sugar, cinnamon and almonds. Put finished cake into pre-heated hot oven. Turn heat off immediately and leave cake in oven for 5 minutes to set meringue. Remove from oven to cool.

FILLING: Melt butter. Add sugar and stir over heat until dissolved. Remove from heat and add cornflour and salt. Stir until smooth. Return to heat and cook gently, stirring all the time. Beat egg-yolk with milk and vanilla. Add to mixture, stirring continuously and cook for 2 minutes. Allow to cool.

TOPPING: Beat egg-whites until stiff and add ½ cup sugar gradually. Beat until smooth. Combine coconut, sugar, cinnamon and almonds in a separate bowl.

Tangy Apricot Cake

4 oz. dried apricots
½ cup water
2½ cups self-raising flour
pinch salt
1¼ cups castor sugar
3 oz. butter
1 egg
5 oz. warm milk

APRICOT BUTTER CREAM
2 oz. butter
1 cup sifted icing sugar
3 tablespoons apricot pulp
1-2 tablespoons milk

Wash apricots, soak in ½ cup water 1 hour. Bring to boil and cook until soft. Drain off liquid. Cool. Sift flour and salt into a bowl and add castor sugar. Make well in centre and beat in softened butter. Add egg, milk and ½ cup apricot pulp. Continue beating 2 to 3 minutes. Place mixture in 2 buttered 7-in. sandwich tins and bake in moderate oven 25 to 30 minutes. When cool, join together and frost with Apricot Butter Cream.

APRICOT BUTTER CREAM: Cream butter, add icing sugar and apricot pulp. Beat until smooth. Blend in milk and spread over cake.

Chocolate Gold Layer Cake

1 cup castor sugar
1 teaspoon vanilla
2 cups plain flour
4 oz. butter
3 teaspoons baking powder
pinch salt
1 cup milk
4 oz. cooking chocolate, grated
3 egg-whites

BUTTER CREAM
6 oz. butter
3 egg-yolks
2¼ cups sifted icing sugar

TOPPING
4 oz. unsweetened cooking chocolate
1 teaspoon butter

Cream butter and half the castor sugar in large basin. Beat in vanilla. Sift dry ingredients and add alternately with the milk to creamed mixture; add grated chocolate. Beat egg-whites until stiff, gradually add remaining castor sugar; beat until mixture is of meringue consistency. Fold meringue into cake batter. Place cake mixture into 3 greased and lined 8-in. sandwich pans and bake in moderate oven for 20 to 25 minutes. Cool 5 minutes in tin before turning out to cool completely. Sandwich cakes together, using half of the prepared icing; cover top and sides with remainder.

BUTTER CREAM: Beat softened butter and egg-yolks together. Gradually beat in sifted icing sugar.

TOPPING: Melt chocolate and butter together in top part of double boiler over hot water. Mix well and carefully drizzle chocolate lines over top and sides of cake.

Peach Kuchen

1 pkt. buttercake mix
½ cup toasted shredded coconut
4 oz. butter
26 oz. can sliced peaches
¼ cup sugar
½ teaspoon cinnamon
1 cup sour cream
1 egg

Combine cake mixture and coconut in basin, cut in butter until mixture resembles coarse breadcrumbs. Lightly press into base and ½ in. up sides of well-greased 8-in. x 12-in. slab tin. Bake in moderate oven 10 to 15 minutes. Arrange well-drained peach slices evenly over the pastry. Combine sugar and cinnamon, sprinkle over peaches. Blend sour cream and beaten egg, pour over peaches. Bake in moderate oven about 10 to 15 minutes, or until topping is set.

Sugar Almond Cake

2 eggs
1 cup sugar
1 teaspoon vanilla essence
1 cup (4 oz.) plain flour
1½ teaspoons baking powder
¼ teaspoon salt
¼ cup top of milk
cornflake crumbs
4 oz. melted butter

SUGAR ALMOND TOPPING
½ cup almonds
¼ cup butter
3 tablespoons sugar
2 teaspoons cream
1 tablespoon plain flour

Beat eggs, sugar and vanilla essence together until light and fluffy. Fold sifted flour, salt and baking powder into egg mixture alternately with top of milk. Add melted butter. Blend until smooth. Butter a 9-in. pie plate and sprinkle with fine cornflake crumbs. Coat well. Spoon batter into pie plate. Bake in a slow oven (325°G, 350°E) for 30 minutes or until cake is cooked. Remove cake from oven. Spread top of cake very gently with Sugar Almond Topping. Return cake to moderate oven and bake 5-10 minutes longer until topping is brown and bubbly. Cut into wedges and serve warm with pineapple or vanilla ice cream.

SUGAR ALMOND TOPPING: Blanch almonds and slice. Combine almonds with butter, sugar, cream and plain flour in a small saucepan. Cook, stirring until mixture begins to bubble. Remove from heat and stir briskly a few times.

Sunny Apple Cake

4 oz. butter
4 oz. castor sugar
2 eggs, well-beaten
2 cups self-raising flour
pinch salt
2 tablespoons milk
16 oz. can pie apples
3 level teaspoons cinnamon
3 level tablespoons sugar

TOPPING
2 level tablespoons brown sugar
2 level tablespoons melted butter
¼ cup plain flour
¼ cup dry bread or biscuit crumbs
¼ cup grated cheese
2 level teaspoons cinnamon

Cream butter, castor sugar until light and fluffy, add well-beaten eggs gradually and beat well. Sift together flour, pinch salt, three times, then fold into butter mixture alternately with milk. Place pie apples in a bowl with cinnamon and sugar, mix together then fold into butter/flour mixture. Place in a greased and floured 8-in. square cake pan and spread evenly. Sprinkle topping over cake mixture in pan and bake for 45 minutes in a moderate oven 350°. Serve hot or cold.

TOPPING: Blend brown sugar into melted butter, then combine with flour, bread or biscuit crumbs, cheese, cinnamon, mix well.

Hussar Cake

1½ cups (6 oz.) self-raising flour
1 cup (4 oz.) plain flour
½ teaspoon bicarbonate of soda
6 oz. butter
1 cup sugar
½ cup red currant jelly
3 eggs
½ teaspoon cinnamon
⅛ teaspoon nutmeg
1 oz. dark chocolate
¾ cup cream
cherry brandy and whipped cream for decorating

Sift together flours and bicarbonate of soda. Cream butter and sugar well, then beat in red currant jelly. Add eggs one at a time, beating well after each addition. Continue beating until mixture is fluffy. Add cinnamon, nutmeg and finely grated chocolate. Stir in the cream alternately with the sifted flour. Place in greased 9-in. ring tin. Bake in moderate oven (350°G, 375°E) 50-55 minutes or until skewer inserted comes out clean. Cool for 10 minutes in tin before turning out. About half an hour before cake is to be served, split the cake into layers and sprinkle the cut surface with cherry brandy, spread whipped cream between the layers, reserving some for the top. Serve as a dessert or cake as desired. Make cake the day before required.

Peach Kuche

Coffee Butter Cake

1 cup sugar
¾ measuring cup water
1 teaspoon vanilla essence
2 large eggs
1½ level tablespoons coffee powder blended with 1 tablespoon sherry
4 oz. butter (soft)
2 tablespoons brown sugar
1½ teaspoons lemon juice
2½ cups self-raising flour—sifted with 1 level tablespoon powdered milk

COFFEE GLAZE
½ cup sugar (scant)
1 tablespoon butter
1 tablespoon coffee powder
1 cup sifted icing sugar
1 teaspoon rum

Use large fluted ring cake tin. Dissolve the sugar in the water over moderate heat. Cool completely. Cream the butter, brown sugar, vanilla and lemon juice. Add the eggs with 2 heaped tablespoons of flour. Beat 2 minutes. Add the cooled liquid and remaining flour in alternate lots, beating smooth after each addition. Stir 5 tablespoons of this mixture into the blended coffee. Butter and flour cake tin, then alternate thin layers of dark mixture with thick layers of light mixture. Bake in moderate oven 45-50 minutes. When cold ice with Coffee Glaze.

COFFEE GLAZE: Boil for one minute sugar, butter and coffee powder. Stir constantly. Partly cool, then beat in icing sugar and rum. Use glaze as soon as it starts to thicken.

Marshmallow Cherry Cake

4 oz. butter
1 teaspoon almond essence
2 eggs
4 oz. chopped glacé cherries
1 cup sugar
2 cups self-raising flour
⅔ cup milk

FROSTING
1 dessertspoon gelatine
½ cup water
1 tablespoon liquid glucose
1 cup sugar
few drops almond essence
4 oz. chopped glacé cherries

Cream butter and sugar with almond essence until light and fluffy. Gradually beat in lightly-beaten eggs. Fold in sifted flour alternately with milk. Stir in chopped cherries. Spoon mixture into greased and lined 9-in. recess cake tin. Bake in moderate oven 40 minutes or until cooked when tested; turn out, allow to cool.

FROSTING: Place sugar, gelatine, water, glucose and almond essence in a small saucepan, stir over low heat until boiling. Boil steadily 2 minutes. Remove from heat, cool, beat until thick and white. Fold in chopped cherries and pile into the cake recess. Allow to set before cutting.

Crunchy Amber Cake

4 oz. butter
1 cup light brown sugar
1 whole egg plus one egg-yolk
1 teaspoon vanilla essence
1½ cups self-raising flour
½ cup milk

FILLING
3 oz. butter
4 level tablespoons light brown sugar
2 level tablespoons cornflour
pinch of salt
1 egg-yolk
1 cup milk
½ teaspoon vanilla essence

TOPPING
2 egg-whites
½ cup white sugar
1 tablespoon coconut
1 tablespoon sugar
1 teaspoon cinnamon
1 tablespoon finely sliced almonds

Cream butter and sugar till light and fluffy. Add eggs and vanilla essence and beat lightly. Fold in self-raising flour alternately with milk, mixing well. Divide mixture evenly in two buttered and floured round sponge cake tins. Bake in a moderate oven 350° for 20 minutes. Turn on to cake cooler when cooked.

FILLING: Melt butter carefully. Add sugar and stir till dissolved. Remove from heat and add cornflour and salt, stir until smooth. Return to heat and cook gently, stirring all the time. Beat egg-yolk with milk and vanilla essence, add to mixture stirring all the time. Cook for 2 minutes. Allow to cool.

TOPPING: Beat egg-whites until stiff and add sugar gradually. Beat until smooth. Combine coconut, sugar, cinnamon and almonds in a separate bowl.

TO ASSEMBLE CAKE: Spread cooled filling between the two round cakes. Spread egg-white mixture of topping on top of cake, then sprinkle combined mixture of topping onto this. Have oven pre-heated to 400° and turn right off. Place cake back in oven for 5 minutes to set the meringue. Remove from oven to cool.

Chocolate Cake Deluxe

8 oz. self-raising flour
¼ teaspoon salt
2 level tablespoons cocoa
1 level tablespoon raspberry jam
1 level tablespoon boiling water
½ teaspoon vanilla essence
4 oz. butter
6 oz. sugar
2 eggs
4 oz. (½ cup) milk

FILLING
4 oz. butter
5 oz. seived icing sugar
½ teaspoon vanilla essence

TOPPING
1 level teaspoon cocoa
1 level tablespoon seived icing sugar
crushed nuts as desired
glace cherries and angelica as desired

Mix cocoa, jam and boiling water to a paste. Add vanilla essence and leave to cool. Sift together flour and salt. Cream butter and sugar together, adding eggs one at a time and beating well after each addition. To this mixture stir in paste of cocoa, jam, etc. Mix well. Stir in the milk, alternately with sifted flour, until mixture is of soft dropping consistency. Place in greased, lined 9-in. cake tin and bake at 375°E, 350°G for 45 minutes or until skewer inserted comes out clean. Cool for 20 minutes before taking out of tin and placing on wire. When quite cold, split cake and insert filling, leaving a little to spread over top of cake and then dredge top with sifted cocoa and icing sugar mixed together. Decorate with crushed nuts, cherries and angelica.

Loganberry Swirls

1½ cups self-raising flour
½ cup milk
4 oz. butter
16 oz. can loganberries

SAUCE
½ cup sugar
½ cup loganberry syrup
1 oz. butter
½ cup white wine

Sift flour, rub in butter and mix to dry dough with milk. Roll out and spread with drained loganberries. Roll up and cut into slices about 1½ in. wide. Arrange in greased casserole. Heat butter, sugar and fruit juice, add wine and bring to boil. Pour over pastry. Bake in hot oven 30 minutes. Serve warm with cream or custard.

Chocolate Orange Mintaire Dessert

3 oz. butter
3 oz. castor sugar
1 teaspoon grated orange peel
2 eggs, well beaten
5 oz. self-raising flour
pinch salt
5 tablespoons milk

FILLING AND COATING
1 cup sugar
4 level tablespoons cornflour
pinch salt
1 egg-yolk
2 tablespoons lemon juice
4 tablespoons orange juice
1½ cups water
2 teaspoons grated orange rind
1 tablespoon butter

SAUCE
1 tablespoon butter
1 tablespoon plain flour
¼ pint water
2 oz. sugar
1 oz. cooking chocolate
2-3 drops peppermint essence (optional)

Beat butter and castor sugar to a cream. Add grated orange peel and gradually add well-beaten eggs. Sift together flour and salt and add alternately with milk to the butter/sugar mixture. Spread evenly in greased and floured 7-in. or 8-in. square cake pan and bake in a moderate oven for 35-40 minutes, or until top springs back when lightly touched in the centre. Cool.

FILLING AND COATING: Blend together sugar, cornflour, salt, egg-yolk, lemon juice, orange juice, water. Blend smoothly and cook over a low heat stirring until mixture is thick. Add grated orange rind and butter. Cool.

SAUCE: Melt butter, blend in plain flour and cook 1 minute. Add water and stir till boiling, add sugar and cooking chocolate, blend well and then add peppermint essence (if desired).

TO ASSEMBLE: Split cake and put together with orange filling. Place on platter and cut into serving portions, separate each portion ½ in. all round from next portion. Spoon or pour orange mixture in between all portions then push them slightly together again. Now completely cover top and sides of cake with orange mixture allowing it to spill on to platter. Trickle chocolate sauce in a design over cake when coating has set. Decorate with a whirl of cream and an orange slice twist.

Date and Walnut Dessert

2 oz. butter
1 cup self-raising flour
pinch salt
1 teaspoon grated lemon rind
½ cup chopped dates
¼ cup chopped walnuts
1 tablespoon brown sugar
1 egg, beaten
¼ cup cold water
½ cup hot water
3 tablespoons golden syrup
1 oz. extra butter

SAUCE
1 cup water
2 tablespoons golden syrup
juice and grated rind of 1 lemon
1 tablespoon cornflour blended with 1 tablespoon cold water
1 oz. butter

Rub butter into sifted flour and salt. Add lemon rind, dates, nuts and sugar. Mix to soft dough with egg and cold water. Place hot water in ovenproof dish and spoon in half mixture, 1 teaspoon at a time. Trickle half golden syrup over, then spoon in remaining mixture. Top with remaining golden syrup and dot with extra butter. Bake in moderate oven 35 to 40 minutes. Serve hot with sauce.

SAUCE: Put all ingredients except butter in saucepan and bring to the boil, stirring. Cook 5 minutes, stirring. Beat in butter. Serve hot.

Loganberry Swirls

Pineapple Dessert Cake

4 oz. butter
¾ cup castor sugar
2 eggs
few drops lemon essence
2 cups self-raising flour
1 teaspoon mixed spice
pinch salt
¼ cup milk
¼ cup pineapple juice drained from 15-oz. can crushed pineapple

TOPPING
½ cup shredded coconut
½ cup brown sugar
1 cup drained crushed pineapple
¼ cup melted butter
10 glacé cherries
2 oz. blanched almonds
½ pint cream, whipped

Cream butter and sugar until light and fluffy. Add eggs one at a time, beating well between each addition. Add lemon essence. Sift flour, salt and spice and fold into mixture alternately with milk and pineapple juice. Put in a buttered lamington tin 11 in. x 7 in. and bake 30 to 35 minutes in moderate oven. Cool slightly before removing from tin.

TOPPING: Combine coconut, brown sugar, drained pineapple and 1½ tablespoons melted butter. Spread over cake. Arrange cherries and almonds on top and brush with remaining melted butter. Set griller to medium heat and grill approximately 4 in. from heat until top is bubbling and almonds toasted. Serve hot with whipped cream or cold decorated with piped cream around edge.

Tasmanian Apple Delight

3 oz. butter
1 cup self-raising flour
2-3 tablespoons cold water

FILLING
½ lemon, cut into 3 slices
½ cup water
¾ cup sugar
2 tablespoons plain flour
¼ teaspoon nutmeg
3 cups apples, peeled and sliced
2 oz. butter

Cut butter into sifted flour until particles are the size of small peas. Sprinkle cold water over mixture and toss lightly with fork until dough is moist enough to hold together. Roll out on floured board to rectangle, 10 in. x 6 in. Cut into triangles or squares. Pour hot apple filling into buttered 9-in. ovenware dish and arrange pastry squares over filling. Bake in moderately hot oven 35 to 45 minutes. Serve with plain or whipped cream.

FILLING: Simmer lemon slices in water until tender, about 5 minutes. Drain water and reserve. Set aside lemon slices. In saucepan combine sugar, flour and nutmeg. Blend in lemon water. Cook until thickened, stirring constantly. Add apples, butter and lemon slices.

Marsala Cassata Delight

2 cups self-raising flour
pinch salt
1 teaspoon bicarbonate of soda
1 tablespoon cocoa
½ cup castor sugar
4 oz. butter
1 egg
1 teaspoon vanilla
½ cup marsala
1 teaspoon vinegar
½ cup warm water

FILLING
1 lb. cottage cheese
¼ cup castor sugar
1 teaspoon vanilla
2 oz. toasted almonds
2 oz. cherries
1 slice glacé pineapple
1 oz. cooking chocolate grated

TOPPING
½ pint cream
1 tablespoon castor sugar
2 oz. cooking chocolate

Sift flour, salt, bicarbonate of soda and cocoa into a basin, add the sugar. Make a well in the centre, add the melted butter, egg, vinegar, vanilla and water; beat until smooth. Divide mixture into two greased and lined 7-in. sandwich tins. Bake in moderate oven 20 to 25 minutes. Allow to stand in the tins for 5 minutes before turning out. Cool cake slightly, then cut each layer in half. Pour marsala over each layer. Fill cake when cold.

FILLING: Sieve cheese. Beat in sugar, vanilla, chopped almonds, chopped cherries, chopped pineapple and chocolate. Spread between each layer.

TOPPING: Whip cream with sugar. Pile on top of cake, decorate with grated chocolate.

Apple Cheese Ring

1 can refrigerated scones (buttermilk or country style)
4 oz. cream cheese, softened
2 oz. butter
1 large apple
1 tablespoon brown sugar
2 oz. slivered almonds

Open scones as directed on can and place round edge of a lightly greased 9-in. sandwich tin. Beat half the butter with cream cheese until smooth, spread over scones. Peel and core apple, slice thinly and place overlapping slices on cream cheese. Mix remaining butter, brown sugar and almonds together and sprinkle over scones. Bake in moderately hot oven for 20 to 30 minutes or until apple is tender. Allow to stand in tin for 5 minutes, then turn out carefully on to cake cooler. These can be served just as they are, as a sweet scone for afternoon tea or supper, or they can be served as a dessert.

Apple Crumble Pie

8 oz. plain flour
4 oz. butter
2 teaspoons sugar
1 teaspoon grated lemon rind
2 drops lemon essence
½ teaspoon cinnamon
¼ teaspoon nutmeg
1 egg-yolk
cold water to mix
red currant jelly

FILLING
5 Granny Smith apples (or 2½ cups tinned apple)
¼ cup white wine (or sherry)
¼ cup honey
1 tablespoon lemon juice
1 teaspoon lemon rind
1 tablespoon golden syrup
½ oz. flour
½ oz. butter
1½ tablespoons chopped almonds
½ teaspoon cinnamon
¼ teaspoon nutmeg
1 egg-yolk
2 egg-whites

CRUMBLE TOPPING
2 oz. butter
4 oz. flour
2 oz. sugar
cinnamon, slivered almonds

DECORATION
cheddar cheese curls (run vegetable peeler down long side of cheese)
red currant jelly (melted)

Rub butter into sifted flour, cinnamon and nutmeg. Add sugar and rind. Combine with egg-yolk, essence and a little water to make a pliable dough. Roll out to fit 9-in. pie plate, crimp edges and brush sides and bottom with red currant jelly (not edges). Spoon filling into prepared pastry, piling higher in centre. Sprinkle topping over filling (keep pie edge clear). Sprinkle crumble mixture lightly with cinnamon and slivered almonds. Cover with alfoil and bake in hot oven 400° for 45 minutes. Remove foil and cook further 15 minutes. Cool. Decorate with a few trickles of jelly and a 'top knot' of cheese curls (this is better done just before serving).

FILLING: Peel and slice apples (or use precooked apple), place in saucepan with wine, lemon juice, rind and honey. Simmer till apples are tender. Stir in golden syrup. Mix flour, cinnamon and nutmeg with a little water and stir in. Stir till thick and smooth. Remove from heat, stir in butter and almonds. Add beaten egg-yolk and cook 1 or 2 minutes longer. Remove and fold in the two beaten egg-whites.

CRUMBLE TOPPING: Mix butter, sugar and flour together till crumbly. Use cinnamon and almonds to sprinkle over crumble.

Apple Ginger Crumble

1 lb. cooking apples
1 oz. butter, melted
1 teaspoon ground ginger
1 cup castor sugar
1 cup plain flour
pinch salt
3 oz. butter
½ cup quick-cooking oats

Peel apples and grate. Mix with melted butter, ginger and ¾ cup castor sugar in a well-buttered pie dish. Sift flour and salt, rub in butter until mixture resembles breadcrumbs. Add remaining sugar and oats, mix well. Sprinkle evenly over apples. Bake in moderately hot oven 30 minutes or until golden and crisp on top. Serve hot with cream.

Lemon Hazelnut Roll

4 eggs, separated
¾ cup castor sugar
1 cup plain flour
4 oz. ground hazelnuts
4 oz. butter
grated rind and juice 1 lemon
few drops sweet sherry
1 cup icing sugar

Butter and line the base of 10-in. x 14-in. shallow tray. Dust lightly with flour and half the quantity of ground hazelnuts. Beat the egg-whites stiffly, add egg-yolks, then beat in castor sugar gradually. Sift flour and add alternately with the lemon juice and rind. Pour into prepared tray and bake in a moderately hot oven 10 to 15 minutes. Turn on to a sheet of greaseproof paper and roll up. Allow to cool completely. Then unroll carefully, spread filling over, re-roll. Cut in slices and serve as a rich dessert cake.

FILLING: Beat the butter to a cream, add the sweet sherry, sifted icing sugar and remaining hazelnuts.

Apple Crumble Pie

Spicy Raisin Pie

1¼ cups plain flour
¼ cup cornflour
pinch salt
4 oz. butter
2 tablespoons icing sugar
1 egg

FILLING

1 cup raisins
water
¾ cup sugar
1 teaspoon cinnamon
½ teaspoon nutmeg
¼ teaspoon ground cloves
salt
2 well-beaten eggs
1 cup cultured sour cream
¼ cup roughly chopped walnuts
1½ teaspoons lemon juice
cream for serving

Sift flour, cornflour and salt, rub in butter. Beat egg and sugar and add to dry ingredients, making a firm dough; knead lightly. Roll out and line greased 9-in. pie plate. Trim edges and pinch into a decorative frill. Bake in hot oven 7 minutes. Pour filling into partly baked pastry shell. Bake in moderate oven 35 to 40 minutes or until set. Decorate with walnut halves and serve with whipped cream.

FILLING: Cover raisins with water, simmer 5 minutes and drain. Combine sugar, spices and salt and add to eggs, beating well but not frothy. Stir in raisins, sour cream, nuts and lemon juice.

Glazed Orange Nut Ring

3 cups self-raising flour
¼ teaspoon salt
1 egg
¾ cup milk
1 dessertspoon sugar
1 tablespoon butter
grated rind of 1 orange
¼ cup honey
½ cup orange juice
½ cup sugar
1 teaspoon cinnamon
1 teaspoon nutmeg
1 teaspoon mixed spice
2 tablespoons melted butter
¾ cup chopped walnuts

Sift flour and salt, rub in the butter. Add sugar and grated orange rind and mix to a scone dough with beaten egg and milk. Turn on to a floured board, knead lightly and cut into 16 pieces. Roll each into a small ball. Butter a deep 8-in. ring tin, pour in combined honey and orange juice. Combine sugar and spices, place mixture on a piece of paper. Dip the balls of dough one at a time in the butter, then roll in the spiced sugar. Pack in layers in the ring tin, sprinkle the balls with chopped walnuts. Place in a hot oven 10 minutes, then reduce heat to moderate; bake further 20 to 25 minutes. Turn on to a hot plate and serve with cream or custard.

Prune Satin Tart

8 oz. self-raising flour
¼ teaspoon salt
1 tablespoon icing sugar
4 oz. butter
1 egg-yolk
½ cup water

FILLING

1½ cups chopped and cooked prunes
3 eggs
⅔ cup brown sugar
½ teaspoon salt
½ teaspoon grated lemon rind
1 cup thick sour cream
2 teaspoons lemon juice
1 cup cream
1 teaspoon vanilla
1 tablespoon sifted icing sugar
1 teaspoon gelatine
¼ cup hot water

Sift together flour, salt and icing sugar. Rub in butter with finger tops until mixture resembles fine breadcrumbs. Beat egg-yolk and water. Add to sifted flour, reserving a little for glazing. Turn on to a floured board and knead lightly. Roll out. Line a 9-in. tart plate. Decorate edges, brush with reserved egg mixture and prick bottom. Bake at 375° for 10 minutes or until golden brown. Cool in tart plate. Spoon filling into pie shell and chill at least 3 hours in refrigerator. Whip cream until it thickens. Add vanilla and sifted icing sugar. Dissolve gelatine in hot water and add to cream and beat well. Pile on to chilled prune filling. Serve cold.

FILLING: Place prunes into a saucepan. Beat eggs and brown sugar until foamy. Add salt, lemon rind and sour cream. Combine with prunes, place over a low heat and cook, stirring constantly until thick. Remove from heat. Cool. Stir in lemon juice.

Gala Macaroon Flan

1½ cups self-raising flour
pinch salt
1½ tablespoons castor sugar
4 oz. butter
1 egg-yolk
1 tablespoon water
1 tablespoon semolina

FILLING
4 oz. butter
½ cup castor sugar
2 egg-yolks
1 cup chopped prunes (soaked in 1 tablespoon rum for several hours)

TOPPING
2 egg-whites
¼ cup castor sugar
2 oz. ground almonds
2 drops almond essence
blanched almonds for decoration

Sift flour, salt and sugar into a basin. Rub in butter. Add egg-yolk and water and mix to a firm dough. Knead on floured board and roll to fit 9-in. flan or springform pan. Sprinkle base with semolina. Spread with filling. Cover with topping, decorate with blanched almonds. Bake in moderate oven 40 to 50 minutes. Serve, if desired, with whipped cream.

FILLING: Cream butter and sugar until light and fluffy, add egg-yolks and the soaked prunes; mix well.

TOPPING: Beat egg-whites until stiff; fold in remaining ingredients except blanched almonds.

Southern Queen Apple Lemon Pie

SNOWFLAKE PASTRY *(original)*
5 oz. (1¼ cups) self-raising flour
5 oz. (1¼ cups) plain flour
(sifted together twice)
¼ teaspoon salt
6 oz. butter, chilled until firm
⅔ cup evaporated milk, well chilled
2 teaspoons strained lemon juice
2 teaspoons grated lemon rind
cream

FILLING
1½ lb. firm apples, peeled and cut into thick slices
3-4 oz. sugar
rind 1 lemon, peeled very thinly
1½ cups water

LEMON BUTTER
½ cup lemon juice strained
1 dessertspoon grated rind
½ cup sugar
2 oz. butter
1 level tablespoon cornflour
1 egg-yolk, slightly beaten

Sift flours on to pastry board, grated chilled butter over flour, mix lightly. Whip chilled milk until thick, fold in lemon juice and rind. Add sufficient cream to make butter and flour into a stiff dough. Roll in oblong strip, damp edges, roll up like a swiss roll. Chill 10 minutes or longer. Roll pastry out to ¼-in. oblong sheet. Cut off ten ½-in. strips. Line a deep pie plate with remainder, brush sides and base with egg-white (unbeaten). Trim edges and decorate. Spread a thick layer of lemon butter over base. Arrange apple slices overlapping over top. Brush apple with lemon butter (melted). Glaze pastry strips, arrange criss-cross over apple. Bake in hot oven (400°G, 450°E) 10 minutes, reduce heat, bake further 10 minutes or until golden brown. Serve cold decorated with whirls of whipped cream, or warm with ice cream or cream.

FILLING: Bring water, lemon rind and sugar to the boil, add apple slices, simmer until tender, but not broken, remove lemon, strain.

LEMON BUTTER: Mix lemon juice, rind and sugar, heat, stir until sugar is dissolved. Stir in cornflour mixed with egg-yolk and little water, cook over hot water until thick, stir in butter.

Pear Delight

1 15-oz. can pears
¾ cup sugar
3 oz. butter
glacé cherries to decorate
2 eggs
¾ cup castor sugar
4 oz. butter, melted
1 tablespoon rum
3 drops lemon essence
grated rind of 1 orange
2 cups self-raising flour
¼ teaspoon salt
½ cup pear juice

Drain pears, reserve juice, and stand pears to dry on a cloth. Put sugar in saucepan over medium heat and allow to melt and become golden. Add butter and stir well with a wooden spoon. Pour into buttered 9-in. round cake tin. Slice pears and arrange with cherries over the caramel. Put eggs and castor sugar into bowl and beat until thick. Pour in melted butter, rum, lemon essence and orange rind. Fold in flour sifted with salt alternately with pear juice. Pour cake mixture over pears and bake 40 minutes in a moderate oven. Turn on to serving plate immediately.

Apricot Dessert Cake

PASTRY
2½ tablespoons custard powder
½ cup self-raising flour
½ cup plain flour
pinch salt
¼ cup castor sugar
3 oz. butter
¼ cup cold milk
2-3 tablespoons apricot jam

CAKE
1½ cups self-raising flour
pinch salt
1 teaspoon cinnamon
3 oz. butter
¼ teaspoon nutmeg
1 egg
½ cup milk
4 oz. glacé apricots, chopped
½ cup sugar

PASTRY: Sift dry ingredients into a basin. Rub in butter, mix to a firm dough with milk. Roll to fit 7-in. x 11-in. lamington tin. Spread with jam.

CAKE: Sift dry ingredients into a basin, add butter, egg, milk and apricots. Beat for 2 minutes; spread over pastry. Bake in hot oven for 30 to 35 minutes. Cut into squares. Serve warm with cream or custard.

Southern Queen Apple Lemon Pie

Apple Glacé Dessert Cake

4 oz. butter
3 oz. sugar
2 eggs, beaten
7 oz. self-raising flour
pinch salt
3 dessertspoons finely chopped mixed peel
1 teaspoon lemon juice
1 teaspoon vanilla essence

WALNUT PASTE
6 oz. walnut pieces
1 egg, beaten
6 oz. castor sugar
sifted icing sugar for dusting

APPLE GLACÉ
3 cups unpeeled apples
6 oz. sugar
2 oz. self-raising flour
1 egg, beaten
2 oz. butter, melted
1 teaspoon vanilla essence

Cream butter and sugar until light and fluffy, gradually add beaten eggs. Sift together flour, salt and add to creamed mixture alternately with mixed peel. Stir in lemon juice and vanilla essence, mix well together. Spread half of mixture in a greased and floured square cake pan (8 in. x 8 in. x 3 in.). Roll out walnut paste on a board dusted with icing sugar to 8-in. square, then place on top of cake mixture in pan. Add rest of cake mixture and top with Apple Glace. Bake at 425° moderately hot oven for 45 minutes. May be served hot or cold.

WALNUT PASTE: Chop or mince walnut pieces very finely and mix together with egg and castor sugar in a small saucepan over a low heat, making a paste, allow to cool.

APPLE GLACE: Dice apples and put into a bowl together with sugar, flour, egg, butter and vanilla essence. A few drops of red food colouring may be added to give a rosy glow (optional). Mix well together and place on top of cake mixture in pan.

French Apple Meringue

1 cup self-raising flour
2 oz. butter
1 oz. castor sugar
water to mix

FILLING
1 lb. cooking apples
3 oz. castor sugar
water
1 tablespoon apricot or plum jam
3 oz. butter
2 eggs, separated
1 oz. desiccated coconut
1½ oz. fresh breadcrumbs
juice of 1 lemon

Sift flour into a bowl. Rub in butter with fingertips or a pastry blender until it resembles fine breadcrumbs. Add sugar and mix to a smooth dough with water. Knead lightly. Roll out and line a buttered 9-in. pie plate. Trim and flute edges. Place a piece of greaseproof paper over pastry and weight it down with dried beans or rice. Bake 15 to 20 minutes in moderately hot oven. Remove paper and beans. Fill with apple filling and bake further 20 minutes in moderate oven.

FILLING: Peel, core and slice apples into a saucepan. Add 1 oz. sugar and a small amount of water. Simmer until tender. Beat well, stir in jam and 1 oz. butter. Pour into partly cooked pastry shell. Cream remaining 2 oz. butter and remaining 2 oz. castor sugar until light and fluffy. Add egg-yolks and beat well. Stir in coconut and breadcrumbs. Add lemon juice and beat well. Beat egg-whites until stiff and fold into mixture. Pile on top of apple.

Tipsy Dessert Cake

4 oz. butter
½ cup castor sugar
2 eggs
½ cup milk
2 cups self-raising flour

FILLING
½ cup (lightly packed) brown sugar
1 oz. butter
1 cup well-drained, sliced stewed apple
½ teaspoon cinnamon
2 oz. chopped raisins
2 oz. currants
2 oz. chopped glacé cherries
3 tablespoons brandy

Butter 8-in. square tin and line base with greaseproof paper. Cream butter and sugar until fluffy. Gradually add beaten egg. Add sifted flour and milk alternately. Put a little more than half the mixture in tin. Spread the cold filling over, cover with remaining cake mixture. Bake in a moderate oven 40 to 45 minutes. Allow to stand in tin a few minutes before turning out, as cake is very light. Serve warm, cut into squares, topped with cream or ice cream.

FILLING: Heat brown sugar and butter until butter melts. Add remaining ingredients, cook gently 3 minutes, and allow to become cold.

Golden Crown Dessert

15 oz. can pineapple rings
15 oz. can apricots
3 large eggs
⅓ cup castor sugar
½ cup plain flour
2 oz. butter, melted
1 teaspoon brandy

CHEESE FILLING
10 oz. cream cheese
1 cup condensed milk
½ teaspoon grated lemon rind
½ teaspoon grated orange rind
1 dessertspoon brandy
⅓ cup lemon juice

PIE JEL
1 dessertspoon gelatine
½ cup reserved apricot juice
1 teaspoon brandy
½ cup reserved pineapple juice
1 teaspoon lemon juice

Drain apricots and pineapple well, reserving the liquids separately. Place fruit on absorbent paper to dry well. Beat eggs, gradually beat in castor sugar, continue beating until thick. Fold in sifted flour, then melted butter. Bake in greased and floured deep 8-in. cake tin in moderate oven 25 to 30 minutes. Cool; split horizontally, sprinkle top half with brandy.

CHEESE FILLING: Beat cheese, add milk and blend until smooth. Add fruit rinds, brandy and lastly, lemon juice. Stand for 5 minutes to thicken.

TO ASSEMBLE CAKE: Sandwich layers together with cheese filling; cover top and sides with filling. Cut 4 pineapple rings in halves and press these, rounded sides up, round base of cake. Decorate top with remaining pineapple rings and apricot halves. Refrigerate for 30 minutes. Spoon Pie Jel over top of cake.

PIE JEL: Soak gelatine for 5 minutes in combined apricot and pineapple juices. Place in saucepan, stir well, bring to the boil. Remove from heat; add lemon juice and brandy. Refrigerate until mixture thickens slightly; carefully spoon over top of cake. Chill well before serving.

Orange Chiffon Tart

1 cup self-raising flour
¼ teaspoon salt
2 oz. butter
1 tablespoon sugar
1 dessertspoon grated orange rind
1 egg-yolk
1 tablespoon orange juice

FILLING
½ cup orange juice
2 tablespoons lemon juice
pinch salt
½ cup sugar
3 egg-yolks
1½ dessertspoons gelatine
4 tablespoons water
1 tablespoon grated orange rind
3 egg-whites
½ cup sugar, extra

Sift flour and salt, rub in butter, add sugar and orange rind. Mix to a dry dough with egg-yolk and orange juice (a little more orange juice may be required). Turn on to floured board, knead lightly, roll to fit 8-in. tart plate. Pinch a frill round edge. Prick base well with fork. Bake in hot oven 12 to 15 minutes. When cool add filling. Refrigerate until set. Decorate with whipped cream and, if desired, chopped walnuts.

FILLING: Combine gelatine and water, set aside. Put orange juice, lemon juice, salt, orange rind, ½ cup sugar and beaten egg-yolks in top of double saucepan; cook over boiling water, stirring until mixture coats a spoon and thickens to custard consistency. Add soaked gelatine and stir while cooking. When beginning to thicken, fold in egg-whites beaten to a meringue consistency with ½ cup sugar.

Apricot Brandy Cheesecake

¾ cup plain flour
¾ cup self-raising flour
3 oz. butter
1 teaspoon cinnamon
1 tablespoon sugar
1 egg-yolk
2 tablespoons water

FILLING
1 lb. cream cheese
4 eggs
1 cup castor sugar
1 teaspoon vanilla
½ cup sour cream
2 tablespoons self-raising flour

TOPPING
2 oz. dried apricots
1 tablespoon sugar
brandy to cover
(stand all ingredients in basin overnight)

Sift flours and cinnamon into a mixing bowl, rub in butter until mixture resembles fine breadcrumbs; stir in sugar. Beat egg-yolk with water, mix into flour, forming a stiff dough, adding more water if necessary. Turn on to a floured board, roll out thinly to line 8-in springform pan. Pour filling into prepared pastry and bake in moderate oven 30 minutes. Reduce heat to very slow, bake further 15 minutes or until custard is set. Allow to cool completely before removing from tin. Refrigerate 24 hours.

CHEESE FILLING: Sieve cream cheese into a basin. Beat eggs until light and frothy, gradually beat in sugar, beating well after each addition. Add vanilla and sour cream. Gradually beat in cream cheese, beating well after each addition. Add flour, beat until smooth.

TOPPING: Sieve all ingredients, mix well and spread over cheesecake. Decorate with whipped cream before serving.

Zitronenauflauf (Lemon Souffle)

3 oz. butter
2 cups milk
1 cup self-raising flour
4 eggs, separated
½ cup castor sugar
½ cup lemon juice
grated rind 1 lemon
2-3 large green apples
1 tablespoon extra sugar
pinch salt

WINE SAUCE
1 cup apple or grape juice
1 egg
1 tablespoon sugar
1 extra egg-yolk

Melt butter over low heat in saucepan, blend in flour and salt; gradually stir in milk. Cook over low heat until smooth and thick. Beat egg-yolks and sugar well, stir into flour mixture. Stir in grated rind and lemon juice. Fold in stiffly beaten egg-whites. Peel and core apples, cut into ⅛ in.-thick slices. Arrange apples on base of large greased souffle dish; sprinkle with extra sugar. Carefully pour batter over apples. Bake in moderate oven 45 minutes. Serve with Wine Sauce.

WINE SAUCE: Place juice, sugar, egg and egg-yolk into saucepan over hot water; beat with rotary beater until thick and frothy. Do not allow to boil. Serve immediately.

Orange Chiffon Tar

Apricot Chocolate Rum Dessert Cake

4 oz. butter
¾ cup castor sugar
2 eggs
3 oz. chocolate, melted and cooled
1 tablespoon rum
¼ teaspoon salt
2 cups self-raising flour
¾ cup milk
¾ cup dried apricots
½ cup boiling water
¼ teaspoon bicarbonate of soda
chopped nuts

APRICOT CARAMEL ICING
¼ cup reserved apricot liquid
½ cup firmly packed brown sugar
2 tablespoons cocoa
3 tablespoons butter
1½ cups icing sugar
1-2 tablespoons rum

Pour boiling water over apricots, cover for 4 or 5 minutes, drain and cut roughly; reserve liquid for icing mixture. Cream butter and sugar until light. Beat in eggs one at a time. Blend in the cooled, melted chocolate and rum. Sift together flour, salt and soda, add alternately to the creamed mixture with the milk, beginning and ending with dry ingredients. Blend in the apricots gently, combine well. Put into well-greased and lightly floured deep 9-in. ring tin or 8-in. round or square tin. Bake in moderate oven 45 to 50 minutes for the ring tin, 55 to 60 minutes for the other tin. Let stand in tin 5 minutes, turn out carefully on to cake cooler. Ice when quite cold with Apricot Caramel Icing.

APRICOT CARAMEL ICING: Put apricot liquid, sugar and cocoa in saucepan. Simmer 2 or 3 minutes over low heat, stirring all the time. Stir in butter, cool. Blend in sifted icing sugar and rum. Spread over top and sides of cold cake. Sprinkle chopped nuts over top and sides.

Pumpkin Cheesecake

¾ cup plain flour
¾ cup self-raising flour
1 dessertspoon castor sugar
3 oz. butter
1 egg-yolk
2 tablespoons cold water

FILLING
4 eggs
1 cup sugar
1 dessertspoon preserved ginger syrup
1 dessertspoon lemon juice
1 lb. cream cheese
1 cup cooked mashed pumpkin
whipped cream to decorate

Sift flours into a basin, stir in sugar. Rub in butter until mixture resembles fine breadcrumbs. Beat egg-yolk with water. Add to flour to form a firm dough. Roll out and line 8-in. springform pan. Pour filling carefully into pastry shell, bake in moderate oven 30 minutes; reduce heat to very slow for further 30 minutes. Cool, then refrigerate, preferably overnight. Decorate with whipped cream before serving.

FILLING: Beat the eggs, add sugar gradually, beating all the time. Sieve the cream cheese, add ginger syrup, mix well. Add pumpkin to cheese mixture; beat in eggs, mixing until smooth; stir in lemon juice.

Apricot Prune Dessert

1 pkt. Luncheon Fruit Cake Mix
½ cup dried apricots
½ cup prunes, stoned
1 tablespoon brown sugar
2 tablespoons butter

FRUIT SAUCE
1 tablespoon butter
1 tablespoon brown sugar
½ cup water
grated rind ½ lemon
1 teaspoon cornflour

Soak apricots and prunes till tender in a little warm water. Drain well and place fruit decoratively on the base of a greased and lined 7" x 2½" deep round cake tin. Sprinkle with brown sugar and dot with butter. Prepare cake mix as directed on the pack, retain fruit for sauce, and spread cake batter over apricots and prunes. Bake in a moderate oven 350°F gas or electric, for 45 to 50 minutes.

FRUIT SAUCE: Melt butter in small saucepan, add brown sugar, lemon rind and retained fruit mixture. Cook gently for 5 minutes. Blend cornflour with water and stir into fruit mixture. Stir till boiling and cook for further 2 minutes.

Apricot Chocolate Rum Dessert Cak

Savoury Cheese-Cream Pie

8 oz. plain flour
4 oz. butter
3 oz. cream cheese
pinch salt
dash cayenne pepper
1 egg-yolk
squeeze lemon juice
little water

FILLING
¼ lb. bacon rashers
2 large onions
4 oz. tasty cheese
1 dessertspoon butter
1 oz. water
3 eggs
¾ cup cream
salt
pepper
pinch nutmeg

Sift flour, salt and cayenne pepper into basin. Rub in butter and cheese until mixture resembles fine breadcrumbs. Add egg-yolk beaten with lemon juice and water. Mix to firm dough. Knead slightly. Roll out and line 9-in. pie-plate. Chill. Turn filling into uncooked pastry base. Sprinkle top with remaining 1 oz. grated cheese. Bake in moderate oven 45 minutes until custard set and pastry nicely brown.

FILLING: Grill bacon until crisp. Crumble and place carefully on pastry. Peel and slice onions, place in water and butter, gently cook until transparent, leave to cool. Beat together eggs and cream, add nutmeg then 3 oz. grated cheese. Fold in onions.

White Tower Savoury Flan

short pastry
small tin anchovy fillets
1 dozen stuffed olives

FILLING
1 large onion, finely chopped
1 dessertspoon butter
1 tablespoon chopped gherkin
¼ pint cream or top milk
2 eggs
8 oz. cottage cheese
salt and pepper to taste

Roll out pastry and line a 7-in. flan ring. Bake in hot oven 10 to 15 minutes. Prepare filling while flan is baking and spoon into the hot flan case. Bake in moderate oven further 20 minutes. Garnish with lattice of anchovy fillets topped with stuffed olives. Serve hot or cold.

FILLING: Fry onion in butter until golden brown. Add gherkin. Mix in cream, well-beaten eggs and cottage cheese. Season to taste.

Savoury Ham and Onion Tart

PASTRY
1½ cups self-raising flour
pinch salt
3 oz. butter
3 oz. cheese, grated
1-2 tablespoons iced water

FILLING
2 large onions, sliced thinly
2 oz. butter
1 dessertspoon plain flour
2 eggs
1 teaspoon dry mustard
salt and pepper to taste
½ cup evaporated milk
1½ cups cooked chopped ham or corned beef
3 oz. cheese, grated

SAUCE
1 cup tomato purée
1 teaspoon chopped parsley
pinch ground oregano
1 teaspoon chopped parsley
pinch garlic salt
salt and pepper to taste

PASTRY: Sift flour and salt, rub in butter until like breadcrumbs. Add cheese and mix to a stiff dough with water, chill 1 hour. Roll out and line a buttered 9-in. tart plate.

FILLING: Fry onions in butter until golden brown. Stir in flour. Beat eggs, mustard, salt and pepper with milk. Cover pastry with onions, then ham, and then cheese. Pour egg mixture carefully over them. Bake in hot oven 15 minutes, reduce to low and cook further 10 minutes until set. Serve with spicy tomato sauce.

SAUCE: Mix all ingredients well together, bring to boil over very low heat.

Savoury Cheese-Cream Pie

Raisin Turnovers with Coffee Cream

(Makes 8 turnovers)
4 oz. seeded raisins
1 teaspoon grated lemon rind
1 tablespoon boiling water
4 oz. self-raising flour
2 oz. plain flour
pinch salt
2 oz. butter
2 tablespoons sugar
1 egg-yolk
4 tablespoons milk
lemon essence
2 tablespoons honey
2 tablespoons lemon juice
1 oz. butter
1 cup hot water

COFFEE CREAM
1 oz. butter
2 tablespoons cornflour
2 tablespoons sugar
2½ cups milk
1 tablespoon coffee essence
1 egg-white

Cut up raisins. Add lemon rind and boiling water. Divide into 8 portions. Sift together flours and salt. Rub in butter and add sugar. Mix egg-yolk and milk and lemon essence and add to flour and form into a firm dough. Roll out thinly and cut out 8 circles 4 in. in diameter. Place raisin mixture on each, moisten edges and fold over and press well together to form turnovers. Place on a well-greased ovenproof dish, leaving room for expansion. Mix honey, lemon juice, butter and hot water. Pour over turnovers. Bake at 375° for 20 minutes. Serve hot with Coffee Cream.

COFFEE CREAM: Melt butter in a saucepan, add cornflour and blend well. Add sugar and milk and stir constantly over heat until it thickens. Boil for 2 minutes, remove from heat and leave for 3 minutes. Add coffee essence and whisk in stiffly beaten egg-white.

Canadian Maple Pie

4 oz. butter
2 oz. castor sugar
1½ cups (6 oz.) plain flour
3 eggs
1 oz. blanched almonds
½ cup maple syrup or ¼ cup golden syrup and ¼ cup water
juice and rind of 2 oranges
1 dessertspoon gelatine
2 tablespoons cold water
2 oz. butter
1 tablespoon brown sugar
1 oz. crystallized ginger
1 oz. crystallized pineapple

Cream together butter and sugar. Mix in flour until crumbly. Add 1 egg-yolk. Knead well. Roll out pastry to fit 8-in. pie plate. Decorate pastry edge and place butter wrapper on base. Cover with almonds to stop pastry rising and to brown almonds for decoration. Bake in a moderate oven (350°G, 375°E) for 10 minutes. Remove almonds and paper and return pie to oven for further 10 minutes. Cool thoroughly. Pour filling into shell. Chill. Decorate with chopped brown almonds and chopped crystallized ginger and pineapple.

FILLING: Heat maple syrup and slowly beat in 2 egg-yolks. Add juice and rind of oranges. Cook in double saucepan stirring until mixture thickens (15 minutes). Remove from heat. Add gelatine which has been softened in water. Stir until dissolved. Beat in butter. Cool. Beat egg-whites until stiff, then beat in brown sugar. Fold into filling.

Apricot Cheese Tartlets

(Makes 2 dozen)

APRICOT FILLING
2 dozen dried apricots
water to cover
¼ cup castor sugar

PASTRY
scant ½ cup icing sugar
scant ½ cup custard powder
6 oz. butter
1½ cups plain flour

CREAM CHEESE FILLING
8 oz. cream cheese
½ cup sugar
2 tablespoons lemon juice
½ teaspoon vanilla
2 eggs
nutmeg

APRICOT FILLING: Cover apricots with water, allow to stand overnight. Next day, drain, place in saucepan with sugar and fresh water to cover; simmer gently until tender. Drain and set aside to cool.

PASTRY: Cream butter and sifted icing sugar; gradually add sifted flour and custard powder. Divide into 24 even sized pieces, press into deep greased patty pans. Prick base of each with fork. Bake in moderate oven 15 minutes. Remove from tins and place on oven tray.

CREAM CHEESE FILLING: Beat cream cheese until smooth, gradually add sugar, eggs, lemon juice, vanilla, beating well until combined.

TO ASSEMBLE: Place an apricot in each case, top with cheese mixture, sprinkle with nutmeg. Bake in very slow oven 25 minutes, or until cheese mixture is set.

Ruby Cheese Tart

4 oz. butter
6 oz. plain flour
pinch salt
1 tablespoon finely chopped celery
1 egg-yolk
1 tablespoon lemon juice
1 tablespoon cold water
breadcrumbs

FILLING
½ cup carrot
¾ cup apple
1 cup beetroot (drained free from vinegar)
4 oz. cream
8 oz. cottage cheese
1 egg, beaten
¼ teaspoon salt
¼ teaspoon pepper
¼ teaspoon mustard
2 oz. grated processed cheddar cheese
1 dessertspoon onion

Rub between tips of fingers butter, plain flour and salt. Add celery. Beat egg-yolk, lemon juice and cold water together and add to the flour mixture to make a firm dough. Sprinkle breadcrumbs on a board and roll out pastry on them. Cut to fit 9-in. pie plate. Bake in a hot oven 450° for 10 minutes. (Pastry case will be part baked only.) Add filling, bake at 350° for 15 minutes. Decorate edge of tart with coloured onion and sliced gherkin or pickles. Serve hot or chilled. To chill, cover with aluminium foil and place in refrigerator.

FILLING: Grate together carrot, apple, beetroot. Add cream to cottage cheese then add all grated mixtures and mix well with beaten egg, salt, pepper and mustard. Add cheddar cheese and onion to mixture.

Fruit and Cheese Tart

(Serves 6-8)
4 oz. butter
1 tablespoon sugar
pinch salt
2 cups plain flour
cold water to mix

8 oz. cream cheese
¼ cup castor sugar
8 oz. apple pulp (or 1 cup apple purée)
1½ cups vanilla yoghurt
¼ cup castor sugar, extra
1 dessertspoon gelatine
2 tablespoons water
1 cup fresh strawberries
whipped cream

Cream butter and sugar until light and fluffy, gradually stir in sifted dry ingredients. Mix to a firm dough with cold water. Turn on to a floured board and roll to fit 9-in. pie plate. Prick base of pastry, bake in hot oven until golden brown (approximately 15 minutes). Allow to cool. Beat cream cheese until smooth, add castor sugar; spread over base of pie shell. Cover with apple pulp. Sweeten yoghurt with extra castor sugar. Soak gelatine in water, dissolve over hot water; fold into yoghurt mixture with strawberries, reserving a few for decoration. Pile on to apple pulp; refrigerate. Decorate with whipped cream and reserved strawberries.

Orange Date Cheese Squares

PASTRY
1½ cups plain flour
scant ½ cup custard powder
2 tablespoons icing sugar
½ teaspoon baking powder
4 oz. butter
2-3 tablespoons milk

ORANGE DATE FILLING
6 oz. dates, chopped
¼ cup orange marmalade
2 tablespoons water
2 tablespoons orange juice
1 dessertspoon cornflour

CHEESE FILLING
2 oz. butter
10 oz. cream cheese
2 eggs
2 tablespoons castor sugar

PASTRY: Sift together flour, custard powder, icing sugar and baking powder into a basin. Rub in butter until mixture resembles fine breadcrumbs. Add sufficient milk to make a stiff dough. Turn on to a floured board, roll out ⅔ of pastry and line greased 12-in. x 9-in. swiss-roll pan. Prick base, bake in moderate oven 10 minutes; cool.

ORANGE DATE FILLING: Place dates, marmalade and water in saucepan. Cook, stirring continually, over low heat until thick. Combine orange juice and cornflour, stir into date mixture; stir over low heat until mixture thickens, cool.

CHEESE FILLING: Cream butter with cream cheese until soft and creamy. Beat eggs and sugar until light and fluffy; gradually add to cream cheese mixture, beating until smooth. Fold in Orange Date Filling.

TO ASSEMBLE: Smooth filling over cooked pastry shell. Cut remaining pastry into long strips, place them diagonally over filling to form a lattice. Bake in moderate oven 35 to 40 minutes. Let cool in tin. Slice while warm.

Orange Pecan Yoghurt Tarts

4 oz. butter
2 oz. sugar
½ cup self-raising flour } *sift together*
1½ cups plain flour
pinch salt
milk to mix
1 egg-yolk

FILLING
½ cup butter
1 cup sugar
2 eggs
2 teaspoons grated orange rind
½ cup yoghurt
1½ cups chopped pecans
1 cup raisins
pecan halves

Beat sugar with egg-yolk. Add melted butter. Add flour and milk alternately until a firm dough is obtained. Roll out on floured board. Cut and fit into tart tins. Fill tart shells ¾ full with filling. Arrange four pecan halves on top of each tart. Bake 40 minutes in moderate oven or until filling is firm. Cool on wire rack. Remove carefully from tart tins. Decorate with whipped cream rosette and sprinkling of chopped nuts.

FILLING: Cream butter and sugar together, beat in eggs, one at a time, beating well after each addition. Stir in orange rind, yoghurt, chopped pecans and raisins.

Cheese Fruit Horns

4 oz. butter
4 oz. cream cheese
1½ cups plain flour
1 teaspoon baking powder
pinch salt
milk for glazing
sugar

FILLING
1 lb. fresh pineapple (weight after peel and core removed)
1¾ cups sugar
3 in. stick cinnamon
juice 1 lemon

GARNISH
whipped cream
glacé pineapple

Cream butter and cheese together. Work in flour, sifted with baking powder and salt, and mix to a firm dough. Roll out on a floured board and cut into strips approximately 10 in. long and ¾ in. wide (depending on size of metal cream horn moulds). Moisten one edge of each pastry strip with cold water. Fix one end of strip to point of metal mould, wind pastry round, overlapping the dampened edge; finish off end of strip neatly. Do not bring pastry right up to top end of mould or it will be difficult to remove from mould when baked. Glaze with milk and sprinkle with sugar. Bake in hot oven 5 minutes; reduce heat to moderately hot, cook further 15 minutes; halfway through baking time, remove from oven and slip the metal moulds from pastry horns so pastry dries and cooks through. Return to oven until cooked; cool. Fill with prepared filling and decorate with whipped cream and pieces of glacé pineapple.

FILLING: Mince fruit. Put fruit and the juice which has been extracted while mincing, sugar, cinnamon and lemon juice into a heavy pan, boil until fruit is transparent and almost all the liquid has been absorbed. Fruit should not be allowed to crystallize. Cool before using.

Cherry Slices

(Makes 16-20 slices)
1 cup plain flour
½ teaspoon salt
1 tablespoon brown sugar
4 oz. butter

TOPPING
1 cup firmly packed brown sugar
6 oz. walnuts, chopped
8 oz. jar maraschino cherries, drained (reserve liquid for icing)
½ cup desiccated coconut
2 eggs, beaten
3 tablespoons plain flour
1 teaspoon baking powder

BUTTER ICING
2 oz. butter
1 cup icing sugar
¼ cup reserved cherry juice

Sift flour and salt into basin, add brown sugar. Rub in butter and work with fingers until mixture clings together. Press into a shallow 8-in. square tin. Bake in hot oven 5 to 10 minutes. Leave in tin, cool slightly. Mix topping ingredients and spread over base. Bake further 30 minutes in moderate oven; cool. Ice with Butter Icing or dust with sifted icing sugar.

BUTTER ICING: Cream together butter and sifted icing sugar; gradually add cherry juice and blend well.

Orange Pecan Yoghurt Tarts

Tuna Pie with Horseradish Cashew-cheese Sauce

2 oz. butter
3 cups cornflakes, crushed
1 small onion
¾ cup celery chopped
1 oz. butter
½ cup plain flour
1 5-oz. can condensed tomato soup
16 oz. can tuna
2 tablespoons lemon juice
1 teaspoon salt
pepper

HORSERADISH AND CASHEW-CHEESE SAUCE
2 oz. butter
2 oz. cheese, finely sliced
¾ cup milk
1 teaspoon dry horseradish
pepper
½ teaspoon salt
1 egg
2 oz. cashew nuts, chopped

Add melted butter to cornflakes; mix well. Press into greased 9-in. pie plate. Sauté chopped onion and celery in melted butter until tender. Add flour slowly, cook few minutes, stir in tomato soup, drained flaked tuna, lemon juice, salt and pepper; stir over low heat until mixture thickens. Pour into crumb crust. Bake in hot oven for 15 minutes. Serve with the sauce.

SAUCE: Melt butter in saucepan, add cheese, milk, horseradish, salt and pepper. When blended add beaten egg. Stir until thick over low heat. Stir in chopped nuts. Serve hot, pour over pie.

Bacon Cheese Wedges

8 oz. ripe tomatoes
2 cups plain flour
1 teaspoon salt
4 oz. butter
6 stuffed olives, sliced

BACON FILLING
8 oz. lean shoulder bacon
1 dessertspoon butter
4 oz. cream cheese
½ teaspoon dry mustard

CHEESE TOPPING
1 egg
½ teaspoon worcestershire sauce
4 tablespoons milk
1 tablespoon finely chopped parsley
4 oz. grated cheddar cheese
salt and pepper to taste

Cut tomatoes in half, rub through a sieve. Sift flour and salt, cut in butter with pastry blender or knife until mixture resembles breadcrumbs. Add sufficient sieved tomato to make a firm dough. Knead lightly and roll out on a floured board and line a buttered 8-in. x 12-in. tin and bake in hot oven 15 to 20 minutes. Spread with Bacon Filling and spoon Cheese Topping over to cover evenly and garnish with olives. Return to slow oven and bake further 10 minutes. When cool cut into wedges.

BACON FILLING: Remove rind and chop bacon finely. Melt butter in frypan and sauté bacon until cooked. Drain, soften cream cheese, blend in mustard then combine with bacon.

CHEESE TOPPING: Beat egg, add worcestershire sauce, milk, parsley, cheese, salt and pepper.

Pizza Pie

(Serves 4-6)
1 can refrigerated scones (buttermilk or country style)
1 oz. butter
1 medium onion
2 tablespoons tomato paste
1 clove garlic
¼ teaspoon oregano
1 large tomato
¼ lb. mozzarella cheese
6 stuffed olives
1 small can anchovies

Roll out scones to ¼ in. thick, place in 8-in. pie plate, overlapping slightly to form a shell. Sauté chopped onion and crushed garlic in melted butter until soft but not brown. Mix together tomato paste and oregano, spread over scones; sprinkle with onion. Cover with tomato slices and sliced cheese. Cover decoratively with sliced olives and anchovies. Bake in moderate oven 35 minutes.

Apple Pie Deluxe

5 oz. butter
8 oz. plain flour
½ teaspoon salt
2 teaspoons lemon juice
7-8 tablespoons cold water

APPLE FILLING

2 egg-yolks, well beaten
¼ cup cream
1½ oz. castor sugar
¼ teaspoon cinnamon
¼ teaspoon nutmeg
1 tablespoon currants
1 oz. cake crumbs
½ lb. cooking apples—peeled, cored and grated
egg-white
1 tablespoon castor sugar
¼ cup finely chopped nuts

Divide butter into four even portions. Sieve flour and salt into mixing bowl and rub in 1 portion of butter. Add lemon juice and enough cold water to give a nice smooth, non-sticky dough. Turn on to a slightly floured board, and roll out to an oblong, about 10 in. x 6 in. Dab small pieces of second portion of butter evenly over top ⅔ dough, leaving a ½-in. margin all round. Sprinkle with flour. Fold the bottom third of the pastry upwards and the top third down to cover it. Seal open edges with rolling pin. Give pastry half a turn (always to the left). Roll out to a rectangle 10 in. x 6 in. Repeat process till all butter is used. Roll out, fold and seal for fourth time without butter. Wrap in alfoil and chill for 30 minutes. After chilling, cut pastry in halves and roll into two pieces, one approximately 10 in. x 5 in., the other approximately 10 in. x 6 in. Place smaller piece on a dampened piece of alfoil and place on to oven slide. Spread filling on this piece of pastry and leave a 1-in. margin all round. Fold larger piece of pastry in halves lengthwise and on folded edge cut out 5 half diamonds (so that when pastry is opened out, there will be 5 full diamond cutouts). Place this piece on top of filling and brush margin with egg-white, and pinch edges together. Brush all surfaces with a little egg-white and place pastry cutouts (still folded in halves) into each cutout diamond, and bake in hot oven 450° for approximately 30 minutes or till golden brown. Remove from oven, dredge surface with castor sugar and brush a 1-in. margin all round edge with egg-white and sprinkle margin with chopped nuts. Serve hot or cold, with ice cream or cream.

FILLING: Mix all ingredients thoroughly together.

Party Patties

(Makes approximately 20 patties)
2 cups self-raising flour
½ teaspoon salt
5 oz. butter
3-5 tablespoons milk
extra milk for glazing

FILLING
3 oz. butter
1 medium onion
2 cloves garlic
1 green chilli
2 teaspoons turmeric
½ cup water
1 teaspoon salt
½ medium cauliflower, cooked
2 medium potatoes, cooked
½ cup cooked green peas

Sift flour and salt into mixing bowl, cut in the butter until mixture resembles fine breadcrumbs. Add the milk gradually until all ingredients adhere together. Refrigerate pastry 30 minutes. Turn on to a floured board, roll out thinly, and cut into rounds 3 in. or 4 in. wide. Place a dessertspoonful of filling in centre of each pastry round. Wet edges of pastry with a little milk, fold over to form semi-circles and press down edges with a fork. Brush pastry with little milk. Make 1 or 2 slits in top of each to allow steam to escape. Place on greased oven tray; bake in very hot oven for 30 minutes.

FILLING: Heat butter and brown sliced onion lightly. Add crushed garlic and finely chopped chilli; brown. Reduce heat, add turmeric and cook 1 to 2 minutes. Add water, chopped cooked cauliflower, cubed cooked potato and salt. Bring to the boil, reduce heat and simmer 30 minutes. Add peas, stir well, cool. Mash slightly.

Brandied Fruit Pie

short pastry
2 tablespoons walnut pieces
1 tablespoon soft white breadcrumbs mixed with 1 dessertspoon sugar
1 small can pear halves, drained
2 tablespoons finely chopped walnuts

FILLING
½ cup chopped mixed fruit
1 tablespoon shredded mixed peel
2 tablespoons brandy
2 oz. butter
½ cup sugar
pinch salt
¼ cup plain flour
grated rind of ½ lemon
1 cup milk
2 egg-yolks, beaten

MERINGUE
2 egg-whites
4 tablespoons sugar

Roll pastry out and line 9-in. pie plate, press in walnut pieces. Bake in hot oven 10 to 15 minutes. Cool, sprinkle with crumb mixture, cover with cut pears. Spoon filling over, spread with meringue, sprinkle with walnuts and bake in moderate oven 35 to 40 minutes.

FILLING: Mix fruit, peel and brandy. Melt butter and sugar. Blend in salt, flour and lemon rind. Add milk and stir until boiling. Cook 1 minute. Cool slightly, add egg-yolks. Stir 1 minute, do not boil. Cool and combine with fruit.

MERINGUE: Whisk egg-whites, add sugar gradually, continue to beat until mixture forms peaks.

Chicken Pies

rich shortcrust pastry
CHICKEN FILLING
2 cups cooked chopped chicken
4 oz. bacon rashers, cooked, or sliced ham, chopped
1 tablespoon chopped parsley
1 small onion, finely chopped
salt and pepper to season
1 cup chicken stock
1 dessertspoon gelatine

Roll pastry to a thin sheet. Line buttered individual deep pie dishes or ramekin dishes with pastry. Fill pie cases with chicken filling and gently pour over the stock. Top pies with remaining pastry. Cut small slits on pie tops. Bake in a hot oven 20 to 25 minutes. Cool. Store in refrigerator until required. Makes 6 small pies.

FILLING: Combine chicken, ham, parsley, onion, salt and pepper. Dissolve gelatine in 3 tablespoons chicken stock and add to hot stock.

Party Pattie

Miniature Pissaladiere

8 oz. short pastry
2 onions, finely chopped
4 oz. butter
6 large ripe tomatoes, peeled
pinch dried rosemary or oregano
½ cup grated parmesan cheese
1 small can flat anchovies, drained
few black olives, pitted and sliced
olive oil

Line 24 tart pans with rolled out pastry. Chill while preparing filling. Sauté onions in 2 oz. butter until golden. Heat remaining butter, add chopped and seeded tomatoes and cook to a thick paste. Add rosemary. Cover bottom of each tart shell with grated parmesan cheese and fill with layers of onions and tomato mixture. Top each tart with strips of anchovies, crossed, and sliced olives. Brush with a little olive oil and bake in moderate oven about 25 minutes or until pastry is golden. Brush again with olive oil and remove from pans. Serve hot.

Golden Cherry Nut Twirl

2 cups self-raising flour
pinch salt
1 tablespoon castor sugar
1 oz. butter
1 egg, beaten
approximately ½ cup milk

TOPPING
2 oz. butter
¼ cup castor sugar
1 tablespoon golden syrup
2 oz. chopped glacé cherries
2 oz. blanched almonds, roughly chopped

Sift flour, salt and sugar into bowl. Rub in butter. Beat egg lightly with milk and mix into flour to make a moist dough. Knead and roll into long sausage shape. Starting from outside, coil into a buttered 7-in. cake tin. Pour topping over coil and bake in moderately hot oven 35 to 40 minutes. Serve warm or cold spread with butter.

TOPPING: Melt all ingredients in saucepan over gentle heat.

Tumby Cheese Plaits

4 oz. butter
2¼ cups self-raising flour
1 teaspoon salt
1 tablespoon sugar
3 oz. tasty cheddar cheese, grated
1 cup milk

Melt butter in 8-in. square pan. Sift flour, salt and sugar. Add grated cheese. Add milk and mix to a dough with a knife. Knead lightly. Roll dough a little larger than size of pan. Cut dough into slices about 1½ in. wide and 4 in. long, then slit each slice twice to within ½ in. of the top. Plait slices. Coat plaits in melted butter by dipping and rolling them in the pan of butter, arranging them side by side. Bake 12 to 15 minutes in very hot oven. Serve hot with berry jam or jelly and cream.

Date Tea Ring

2 cups self-raising flour
pinch salt
2 oz. butter
2 tablespoons sugar
½ cup chopped dates
1 egg-yolk, beaten
¾ cup milk
egg-white for glazing
1 tablespoon brown sugar

FILLING
1 oz. melted butter
¼ cup brown sugar, firmly packed
2 tablespoons chopped walnuts
1 teaspoon cinnamon

Sift flour and salt, rub in butter. Add sugar and dates. Mix to a soft dough with egg-yolk and milk. Roll out to ¼-in. thickness on floured surface and spread filling over. Moisten edges with egg-white, roll up lengthwise, pressing edges together to form a ring. Slash at 1 in. intervals. Brush top with egg-white and sprinkle with brown sugar. Place on a buttered tray and bake in hot oven 20 to 25 minutes.

FILLING: Mix all ingredients well together.

Luscious Walnut Tea Cake

2 oz. butter
⅓ cup sugar
1½ cups self-raising flour
1 egg
1 dessertspoon cornflour
½ cup milk
1 tablespoon brown sugar
½ cup chopped walnuts
1 teaspoon mixed spice
1 dessertspoon jam
2 tablespoons self-raising flour
1 tablespoon butter
pinch salt

Cream butter and sugar, add egg, beat well. Sift together flour, salt and cornflour. Add to creamed mixture with milk. Put half mixture into greased 8-in. sandwich tin. Mix together brown sugar, walnuts, spice, flour, salt; stir in jam and softened butter. Sprinkle half this mixture over batter in tin. Cover with remaining batter, sprinkle with remaining walnut mixture. Bake in moderate oven 30 to 35 minutes. Serve warm, buttered.

Brandied Almond Apricot Pie

1 cup plain flour
1 tablespoon castor sugar
¼ teaspoon salt
5 oz. butter
1 lb. 13 oz. tin apricots (drained)
2 cups liquid from apricots
½ cup brown sugar
¼ teaspoon cinnamon
¼ teaspoon nutmeg
2 eggs
1 cup sour cream
½ cup ground almonds
1 tablespoon arrowroot
1 tablespoon brandy
2 drops almond essence

Combine flour, castor sugar, salt in a bowl, rub in butter and mix until crumbly. Pat evenly over bottom and sides of a 9-in. springform tin. Arrange apricots on bottom, reserve three for decorating. Mix brown sugar, cinnamon and nutmeg together, sprinkle over apricots. Bake in a hot oven for 15 minutes. Remove and stand aside. Beat eggs until thick. Fold in sour cream and ground almonds. Spoon over hot apricots. Bake in low oven for 25 minutes until custard is set. Heat reserved liquid in saucepan, bring to boil. Thicken with arrowroot mixed with a little water. Cool. Add brandy and almond essence. Decorate with ½ cup whipped cream and apricots.

Spiced Apricot Bread

8 oz. dried apricots
1 cup water
¾ cup castor sugar
3 oz. butter
½ teaspoon cinnamon
½ teaspoon mixed spice
½ teaspoon nutmeg
2 cups plain flour
1 teaspoon bicarbonate of soda
pinch salt
2 eggs, beaten

Cut apricots into small pieces and simmer for 10 minutes in saucepan with water, sugar, butter and spices. Allow to cool. Sift flour, bicarbonate of soda and salt and stir into cooled mixture. Beat in eggs, then spoon mixture into buttered loaf tin (9 in. x 5 in. x 3 in.) and bake in moderate oven about 1 hour. When cool, serve sliced and buttered.

Harlequin Fruit Loaf

2 cups plain flour
1½ teaspoons baking powder
½ teaspoon bicarbonate of soda
½ teaspoon salt
4 oz. butter
⅔ cup firmly packed brown sugar
3 eggs
½ cup sweet sherry
½ cup sieved cottage cheese
½ cup finely chopped dried apricots
½ cup finely chopped prunes

Sift together flour, baking powder, bicarbonate of soda and salt. Cream butter and sugar until light and fluffy. Add eggs one at a time, beating well after each addition. Fold in flour mixture alternately with sherry and blend well. Stir in cheese and fruit. Spoon into a buttered loaf tin (9 in. x 5 in. x 3 in.) lined with quilted aluminium foil and bake in moderate oven 1 hour or until cooked in centre.

Honey Nut Loaves

4 oz. butter
1 cup honey
2 eggs
⅓ cup milk
2 cups plain flour
2 teaspoons baking powder
1 cup sultanas
¼ cup chopped raisins
¼ cup chopped walnuts

Cream together butter and honey. Add eggs one at a time, beating well after each. Add the milk and sifted dry ingredients alternately. Gently stir in raisins, sultanas and walnuts. Butter and flour 2 small nut roll tins and divide mixture evenly between them. Bake in a moderate oven 50 to 60 minutes.

Brandied Almond Apricot Pie

Golden Apricot Slice

1 cup plain flour
½ cup self-raising flour
pinch salt
½ teaspoon cinnamon
½ teaspoon nutmeg
½ teaspoon spice
4 oz. butter
¼ cup golden syrup
2 tablespoons apricot syrup
4 oz. cream cheese
1 tablespoon rum
1 tablespoon cream

FILLING
½ cup brown sugar
4 dessertspoons cornflour
1 tablespoon butter
1 cup apricot syrup
1 small tin apricot halves

TOPPING
1 cup chilled cream
1 tablespoon icing sugar
1 egg-white (stiffly beaten)
few drops almond essence

Sift flours and dry ingredients. Rub in butter. Mix to a firm dough with syrup and apricot juice. Press mixture into shallow cake tin, bake at 400° for 10-12 minutes. Cool. Beat cream cheese until smooth then add rum and cream. Spread this over cooked base, cover with chilled apricot filling. Chill.

FILLING: Combine sugar and cornflour with apricot syrup (make up to 1 cup if not enough). Place over low heat, add butter. Cook gently for 10 minutes. Fold in chopped apricots, cook until mixture is thickened. Cool filling then chill.

TOPPING: Combine all ingredients. Cut dessert in squares, top with cream and decorate as desired. I like apricot halves or slivered almonds.

Italian Scones

(Makes 10)
1 can refrigerated scones
(buttermilk or country style)
3 oz. gruyere or mozzarella cheese
5 anchovy fillets
10 stuffed olives

SAUCE
2 oz. butter
1 medium onion
1 clove garlic
4 tablespoons tomato paste
½ teaspoon oregano
salt, pepper to taste

Place scones on greased oven tray. Make a deep well in each scone and fill with sauce. Cover with grated cheese, top each with anchovy fillet half and sliced stuffed olive. Bake in hot oven 15 to 20 minutes.

SAUCE: Melt butter, add chopped onion and crushed garlic, sauté until soft. Stir in tomato paste and seasonings.

Sweet Bread Twist

2 oz. butter,
2 cups plain flour
¼ teaspoon salt
2 tablespoons sugar
½ oz. compressed yeast
½ teaspoon sugar
5 oz. warm milk
1 egg
extra butter

GLAZE
1 dessertspoon butter
1 tablespoon icing sugar
1 teaspoon honey

Rub butter into sifted flour and salt. Add sugar. Cream yeast with ½ teaspoon sugar, add to warm milk with lightly-beaten egg. Mix into flour to make a light dough. Put into buttered bowl and place in a warm place until doubled in size. Knead and form into a roll 24 in. long. Wind roll into an 8-in. buttered cake tin, beginning at outside, prove in warm place 10 to 15 minutes. Brush glaze over and bake in hot oven 10 minutes, reduce heat to moderate and bake further 10 to 20 minutes. Serve warm with butter.

GLAZE: Mix all ingredients in small saucepan over low heat until melted.

Golden Apricot Slic

Viennese Cream Cheese Pastry

4 oz. plain flour
4 oz. butter
4 oz. cream cheese
2 lb. apples
2 tablespoons brandy (or any white wine)
3 oz. sugar
2 oz. sultanas
1 oz. currants
juice and grated rind of half a lemon
1 egg-yolk beaten with 1 tablespoon of water

Sift flour into bowl, chop in butter and then stir in cheese. Press into a ball shape, but do not knead. Cover and chill for 3/4 hour. Peel, core and quarter apples. Mix with wine, sugar, fruits and juice and rind of lemon. Simmer gently until apples are soft. Roll pastry out on to a floured board, put cold filling in, lengthwise. Moisten edge and fold over into roll. Pinch edges and place, join side down, on a greased oven tray. Brush surface with egg and water and cook in a hot oven (400°) for 30 minutes. When cold, cut into slices and serve with cream.

Cherry Walnut Raisin Loaf

4 oz. butter
¾ cup brown sugar
2 eggs, well beaten
2 cups plain flour
½ teaspoon salt
1 teaspoon cinnamon
1 teaspoon bicarbonate of soda
½ cup sour milk (1 teaspoon vinegar will sour the milk)
1 cup finely chopped raisins
½ cup finely chopped walnuts
6 finely chopped glacé cherries, plus 10 for decoration
angelica

Cream butter and sugar, add well-beaten eggs. Sift flour, salt, cinnamon and bicarbonate of soda twice and fold into creamed mixture alternately with sour milk. Fold in fruits and nuts and a little extra milk if necessary. Place in 8-in. round cake tin lined with buttered foil. Decorate with 10 cherries. Bake in moderate oven 40 to 45 minutes. Turn on to cake cooler. When cool, arrange strips of green angelica around cherries to represent leaves.

Potato Tea Cake

1 oz. butter
½ cup hot mashed potato
1 cup sugar
1 egg, beaten
2 cups self-raising flour
¾ cup milk
few drops lemon essence
pinch nutmeg
½ cup sultanas

TOPPING
1 cup plain flour
1 cup sugar
4 oz. melted butter
pinch nutmeg

Beat butter into hot potato. Add remaining ingredients in order given. Put mixture into 8-in. buttered cake tin. Sprinkle topping over and bake in moderate oven 20 to 30 minutes.

TOPPING: Sift flour into bowl, add sugar, nutmeg and mix in butter until crumbly.

Almond Wedges

1½ cups plain flour
¼ cup ground almonds
½ cup sugar
½ teaspoon salt
4 oz. softened butter
2 egg-yolks, lightly beaten
1 teaspoon lemon juice
egg for glazing
icing sugar

Combine flour, almonds, sugar, salt and butter. Add egg-yolks and lemon juice. Knead until dough forms a ball. Chill 2 hours. Roll out thinly and cut into 3-in. circles, cut each into 4 wedges. Brush with egg glaze and sprinkle with icing sugar. Bake on buttered and floured baking trays in moderately hot oven 6 to 8 minutes.

Viennese Cream Cheese Pastry

Cherry Cheese Squares

2 oz. butter
2 tablespoons castor sugar
⅜ cup self-raising flour
⅜ cup plain flour
1 teaspoon vanilla
pinch salt
1 egg

CHERRY CHEESE FILLING
2 4-oz. packets cream cheese
1 can condensed milk
⅓ cup lemon juice
½ teaspoon vanilla
1 can cherries
1 tablespoon sugar
1 tablespoon cornflour

Cream butter, add sugar gradually, beat in egg and vanilla, beat well. Sift flours and salt together, stir into creamed mixture. Turn on to floured board, knead lightly; chill ½ hour. Roll out to about ⅛ in. thickness. Place in lightly greased 7-in. x 11-in. tin, prick well, bake in moderately hot oven 15 minutes.

CHERRY CHEESE FILLING: Beat cheese 10 minutes, add condensed milk, beat 15 minutes, then add lemon juice and vanilla; pour over base. Drain cherries; remove stones. Add sugar and cornflour to cherry juice, cook slowly, stirring until thickened. While hot pour over cream cheese. Decorate with the cherries; refrigerate. Cut into small squares to serve.

Cream Cheese Apple Strudel

(Serves 6)
4 cooking apples
4 oz. butter
3 tablespoons soft white breadcrumbs
3 oz. sultanas
½ cup sugar
finely grated rind of 2 lemons
2 oz. blanched almonds, coarsely chopped

PASTRY
8 oz. unsalted butter
8 oz. cream cheese
2 cups plain flour

Peel, core and quarter apples, cut into thin slices. Melt 2 oz. butter in saucepan and gently sauté breadcrumbs until golden. Melt remaining butter. Roll pastry out thinly on floured tea towel to an oblong shape. Brush with melted butter. Spread apples on pastry and sprinkle with sultanas, sugar, golden breadcrumbs and grated lemon rind. Fold in edges, roll up pastry, using a tea towel as an aid. Transfer to lightly-buttered oven tray. Brush with more butter. Bake in moderate oven 30 minutes until light golden in colour. Brush with any remaining butter, sprinkle almonds over and bake further 10 minutes or until golden all over. Serve warm with cream or custard.

PASTRY: Cream butter and cheese. Work in sifted flour to make a stiff dough. Chill 2 hours.

Peach Rollups

2 oz. butter
½ cup orange juice
½ cup sugar
1 teaspoon grated orange rind
2 cups self-raising flour
pinch salt
⅓ cup butter, extra
½ cup milk
16 oz. can sliced peaches, well drained
1 tablespoon melted butter
⅓ cup brown sugar
1 teaspoon cinnamon

Simmer together 2 oz. butter, orange juice, rind and sugar for 5 minutes. Pour half this mixture into a buttered 9-in. square ovenproof dish. Sift flour and salt into a bowl, rub in ⅓ cup butter, then add milk to make a soft dough. Roll dough to a 10-in. x 14-in. oblong, brush with melted butter, sprinkle with cinnamon and brown sugar. Place peaches on top and roll up mixture like jam roll. Cut in slices about 1 in. thick with a sharp knife, arrange in syrup, pressing slices lightly until they touch; pour remainder of syrup over. Bake in hot oven 25 to 30 minutes or until nice and crisp on top. Serve with whipped cream.

Cherry Cheese Pie

2 oz. butter
3 dessertspoons castor sugar
1 egg
1 cup plain flour
½ teaspoon baking powder
pinch salt
1 can pie cherries

FILLING
2 4-oz. packets cream cheese
¾ cup castor sugar
2 eggs
2 dessertspoons lemon juice
1½ cups milk
3 dessertspoons flour, sieved
cinnamon

Cream butter and sugar, add egg then mix in sifted flour, baking powder and salt. Pat mixture evenly on to base and sides of a buttered 8-in. square pan. Keep dusting hands with flour to prevent crust mixture from sticking. Spread pie cherries over crust, using type of cherries that have cornflour already added and are ready for baking. Spoon cream cheese filling carefully over cherries so that they do not rise to the top. Sprinkle top lightly with cinnamon and bake in a moderate oven 50 to 60 minutes. Allow pie to cool in oven 30 minutes with heat turned off. Cool, then chill.

FILLING: Mix together cheese and sugar and beat in eggs, one at a time. Add lemon juice, then milk and flour alternately.

Sherry Pumpkin Pie

1½ cups (6 oz.) plain flour
pinch salt
4 oz. butter
1 egg-yolk
2 tablespoons water
1 teaspoon lemon juice

FILLING
2 eggs separated
½ cup firmly packed brown sugar
1 teaspoon cinnamon
½ teaspoon ground cloves
pinch ground ginger
pinch nutmeg
pinch salt
¾ cup milk
¼ cup sweet sherry
1 cup dry mashed pumpkin

Sift together flour and salt. Rub butter into flour, mix to a stiff dough with egg-yolk, water and lemon juice. Knead lightly, roll out pastry on floured board to fit an 8-in. or 9-in. pie plate. Pour filling into uncooked pie shell and bake in a hot oven (400°G, 425°E) for 10 minutes. Reduce heat 50° and cook a further 20-30 minutes or until filling has set. Serve hot or cold topped with whipped cream and chopped nuts.

FILLING: Beat egg-yolks, sugar, spices and salt together until smooth. Add pumpkin, milk and sherry. Beat egg-white until stiff. Fold into pumpkin mixture.

Buttersnow Tartlets

4 oz. butter
2 oz. pure icing sugar
1 egg
¼ teaspoon salt
1 cup (4 oz.) self-raising flour
½ cup (2 oz.) plain flour
2 oz. cornflour

BUTTERSCOTCH FILLING
3 tablespoons butter
1 cup brown sugar
2 tablespoons plain flour
1 egg-yolk
1 cup milk
¼ teaspoon salt
few drops vanilla essence

SNOW WHITE CREAM
2 tablespoons butter
2 tablespoons sugar
2 tablespoons milk
2 tablespoons boiling water
½ teaspoon vanilla essence

Cream butter together with icing sugar, add egg and salt, beat well. Sift flours and cornflour together twice. Combine flour mixture with cream mixture gradually until soft dough is formed. Turn on to a lightly floured board, knead, roll out to ⅛-in. thickness. Cut out circles with a fluted cutter, fit into greased patty pans, prick well. Bake in a moderate oven 350°-375° for 10-12 minutes. Spoon about 1 teaspoon Butterscotch Filling into each tart shell, with a star tube pipe cream on top of each tartlet.

BUTTERSCOTCH FILLING: Melt butter in a saucepan, add brown sugar over low heat, dissolve carefully. Remove from heat, add flour, mix well until smooth. Beat egg-yolk, stir in milk then add gradually to butter mixture, add salt, return to heat and bring to the boil stirring all the time until thick. At the last add a few drops of vanilla essence.

SNOW WHITE CREAM: Cream butter, sugar together thoroughly, add milk drop by drop, beating well all the time. Add boiling water gradually, beat well, flavour with vanilla essence.

Cheese Dreams

4 oz. butter
4 oz. cream or cottage cheese
1½ cups plain flour
1 teaspoon baking powder
pinch salt
milk for glazing
sugar
icing sugar

FILLING
4 oz. currants
2 oz. candied lemon peel
⅓ cup brown sugar,
grated rind and juice of 1 small lemon
1 oz. butter

Cream butter and cheese together. Work in flour, sifted with baking powder and salt, and mix to a firm dough. Roll out on floured board and cut into 4-in. rounds. Put 1 teaspoon of filling on each round. Moisten edges and fold over in halves, pinch together. Glaze with milk and sprinkle with sugar. Make a cut in top of each and bake in a hot oven 20-25 minutes. Cool and dust with icing sugar.

FILLING: Combine currants, lemon peel, brown sugar, lemon juice and rind. Add melted butter. Mix well.

Walnut Butter Bread

½ oz. compressed yeast
pinch sugar
about ¼ pint milk
1 egg
2 cups plain flour
1 teaspoon mixed spice
1 teaspoon salt
¼ cup sugar
1 oz. butter
2-3 oz. melted butter
1 dessertspoon honey
1 cup chopped walnuts

Cream yeast with pinch sugar, add warmed milk, then beaten egg. Sift flour, spice and salt. Add sugar. Make well in centre, stir in yeast and 1 oz. warmed butter. Knead to a smooth dough on lightly-floured surface. Put into a clean, well-buttered bowl, cover and leave in warm place until doubled in bulk. Knead and cut into 3 pieces. Roll into balls, tossing each one in melted butter and honey, then into walnuts. Place in buttered 8-in. ring tin. Put in warm place to prove 20 minutes. Bake in moderate oven 15 to 20 minutes. Serve warm or cold spread with butter.

Easy Marbled Gugelhupf

3 oz. butter
½ cup castor sugar
½ teaspoon vanilla
3 eggs, separated
1½ cups self-raising flour
4 tablespoons milk
2 oz. cooking chocolate, melted
1 tablespoon finely sifted soft white breadcrumbs
icing sugar

Cream butter, sugar and vanilla. Beat until light and fluffy, add egg-yolks, one at a time, beating well after each. Fold in sifted flour alternately with milk. Beat egg-whites stiffly and fold into mixture. Add melted chocolate to $\frac{1}{4}$ of the mixture. Put half white mixture into small buttered gugelhupf ring mould which has been sprinkled with breadcrumbs. Cover with chocolate mixture and top with remaining white mixture. Bake in moderate oven about 40 minutes. Turn out on to cake cooler and dust with icing sugar.

Muffin Rolls

2¼ cups milk, scalded
2 teaspoons salt
4 oz. butter
2 dessertspoons sugar
1 oz. compressed yeast
¼ cup lukewarm water
5 cups plain flour, sifted

Combine milk and salt, cool to lukewarm. Cream butter and sugar together, add to milk. Soften yeast in lukewarm water, stir and combine with milk mixture, add flour and beat until smooth. Put in buttered bowl, cover and let rise in a warm place about 1 hour or until doubled in bulk. Stir down dough, half fill buttered muffin pans, cover and let rise about 45 minutes or until doubled in bulk. Bake in hot oven 15 to 20 minutes.

Cheese Dreams

Walnut Scones

4 cups self-raising flour
1 teaspoon salt
4 oz. butter
2 tablespoons castor sugar
2 oz. chopped walnuts
2 tablespoons warm honey
approximately 1¼ cups milk
extra milk or beaten egg for glazing
extra walnuts to decorate
butter or cream for serving

Sift flour and salt into basin, rub in butter lightly. Stir in sugar and walnuts. Make well in centre, spoon in honey and enough milk to give a firm, but not sticky dough. Knead lightly on floured board and roll out ½ in. thick. Cut into small rounds, place on buttered trays, close together. Brush tops with glaze and put walnut piece on each. Bake in hot oven 7 to 10 minutes until well-risen and golden. Serve hot with butter or cream.

Toasted Almond Loaf

2 oz. butter
1 cup coarsely chopped blanched almonds
1 cup self-raising flour
1 teaspoon salt
½ cup castor sugar
1½ cups wholemeal flour
½ cup brown sugar
1 egg
1¼ cups milk
4 oz. melted butter

Heat 2 oz. butter in small pan, add almonds and fry gently until golden. Sift self-raising flour, salt and castor sugar. Mix in wholemeal flour, brown sugar. Combine beaten egg, milk and melted butter with almonds and the butter in which they were browned. Make well in centre of dry ingredients and add liquid all at once. Mix together lightly, then pour into buttered, paper-lined loaf tin. Bake in slow oven about 1 hour 25 minutes. Cool 10 minutes before removing from tin. Serve in slices with butter.

Apricot Walnut Loaf

2 cups plain flour, sifted
2 teaspoons baking powder
½ teaspoon bicarbonate of soda
½ teaspoon salt
⅔ cup sugar
grated rind of 2 oranges
⅔ cup coarsely chopped walnuts
1 cup coarsely chopped dried apricots, cooked and sweetened
1 egg
¼ cup syrup from cooked apricots
⅓ cup orange juice
¼ cup melted butter

Sift dry ingredients into bowl. Add orange rind, walnuts and apricots and mix to coat. Beat egg with apricot syrup and orange juice. Pour liquid ingredients into dry and fold until well blended. Do not over-mix. Add melted butter and mix well. Spoon into buttered and floured loaf pan (9 in. x 5 in. x 3 in.) and bang on table to expel any air bubbles. Bake in moderate oven 50 to 60 minutes or until loaf tests done. Remove from oven, stand in pan 5 minutes, then loosen edges with dull knife and turn out on to wire cooler. Serve sliced with freshly whipped butter or cream cheese beaten to a fluff with cream and a dash of cinnamon.

Banana Butter Kisses

8 oz. butter
1 cup icing sugar
3 tablespoons mashed banana
few drops vanilla
pinch salt
10 oz. sifted plain flour
4 oz. chopped almonds

CREAM CHEESE FILLING
4 oz. cream cheese
2 tablespoons sifted icing sugar
1 tablespoon chopped glacé cherries

Cream butter, add icing sugar and beat until light and fluffy. Blend in the mashed banana, vanilla and salt. Add the sifted flour and mix in well. Stir in almonds, wrap in greaseproof paper and chill for 1 hour for easier handling. Shape into balls, using rounded teaspoon for each. Place on an ungreased tray; flatten with the bottom of a glass dipped in sugar. Bake in a moderate oven (350°-400°E) 10 to 15 minutes. Cool. When cold join together with Cream Cheese Filling.

CREAM CHEESE FILLING: Soften the cream cheese, blend in icing sugar and beat well. Fold in chopped cherries. Spread between biscuits so as to form kisses.

Mocha-Pecan Jewels

1 cup butter
6 oz. cream cheese, softened
2 cups plain flour
⅛ teaspoon salt
1 cup coarsely crushed rice bubbles

FILLING
2 eggs
1 cup brown sugar, plus 1 tablespoon
1 dessertspoon instant coffee
⅛ teaspoon salt
3 tablespoons cream
1 teaspoon vanilla
1¼ cups coarsely chopped pecan nuts

TOPPING
Whipped unsweetened cream and a dusting of cinnamon

Allow butter to soften at room temperature. Add cream cheese and beat until smooth. Add sifted flour and salt gradually, and beat well after each addition of flour. Work with fingers until it is a smooth dough. Lastly add the coarsely crushed rice bubbles and knead slightly, until they are well mixed in. Break off small pieces of dough and shape into small balls. Place each ball in a well-greased gem iron and press with the thumb so as to line the bottom and the sides of the gem irons or use small patty tins if desired. Sprinkle the pecan nuts in the lined pastry cups. Spoon the filling over the pecans, filling each cup to just below the top of the pan. Bake in a moderate oven 350° for about 20 minutes or until pastry is delicately browned and filling is set. Before serving, top each tartlet with a small rosette of whipped cream and dust very lightly with cinnamon (just a suspicion of cinnamon).

FILLING: Beat eggs slightly. Mix sugar, coffee and salt together. Add gradually to the eggs, beating well after each addition until mixture is completely smooth and blended. Lastly add cream and vanilla and mix in.

Hazelnut Triangles

1¼ cups self-raising flour
pinch salt
2½ oz. butter
1 egg
vanilla
apricot jam

FILLING
3½ oz. butter
½ cup castor sugar
2 tablespoons water
vanilla
4 oz. ground hazelnuts
4 oz. chopped hazelnuts

ICING
½ cup sifted icing sugar
3 teaspoons cocoa
1 teaspoon melted butter
3 teaspoons hot water

Sift flour, salt together. Rub in butter until mixture is like breadcrumbs. Add egg and vanilla. Mix until a soft dough is formed. Turn out on to a lightly-floured board and roll to fit a greased swiss roll tin. Spread a layer of apricot jam over the pastry. Spread filling evenly on jam-coated pastry. Bake in a moderate oven 30 to 35 minutes. Cool slightly. Cut into triangular shapes and cool thoroughly on a wire rack. Sift together icing sugar and cocoa. Add melted butter and water and mix until smooth. Coat two corners of each triangle. Allow to set.

FILLING: Heat butter, sugar, water and vanilla together and bring to boil. Allow to cool. Add ground and chopped hazelnuts. Prepare nuts by roasting in moderate oven for 15 to 20 minutes. Then rub in a tea towel to remove skins.

Lemon Wafers

(Makes 24)
3 oz. butter
⅓ cup castor sugar
1 teaspoon grated lemon rind
1 egg
2 cups self-raising flour
pinch salt
1 tablespoon grated lemon rind mixed with 1 tablespoon sugar

LEMON CREAM FILLING
2 oz. butter
1 cup icing sugar
1 teaspoon grated lemon rind
water

Cream butter and sugar with lemon rind until light and fluffy. Add egg and blend in. Sift flour with salt and add gradually to form a dough. Knead lightly and chill 1 to 2 hours. Roll out thinly and cut into rounds with biscuit cutter. Put on buttered baking trays and sprinkle half with lemon rind and sugar. Bake in moderate oven 10 to 12 minutes. Cool. Join together with Lemon Cream Filling.

LEMON CREAM FILLING: Cream butter and icing sugar, add lemon rind and mix to a spreading consistency with water.

Mocha-Pecan Jewel

Brandy Creams

6 oz. plain flour
4 oz. butter
2 oz. sugar
1 egg-yolk
1 tablespoon cream or evaporated milk
1 dessertspoon brandy

FILLING
1 egg
1 tablespoon castor sugar
1 tablespoon cornflour
1 cup milk
¼ pint cream or evaporated milk (less 1 tablespoon taken out for biscuits)
½ teaspoon vanilla
black coffee
1 teaspoon brandy

ICING
1 tablespoon cocoa
1 dessertspoon butter
3 tablespoons hot water
6-8 oz. sifted icing sugar
vanilla essence
pinch cream of tartar

Sift flour, rub in butter and then add the sugar. Mix the egg-yolk with cream or evaporated milk and the brandy. Stir into flour and mix to a firm dough. Knead a little on a lightly floured board. Roll as thinly as possible and cut into small rounds with a floured cutter. Bake on greased oven trays in a hot oven (400°G, 450°E) for 7 minutes. When cold, top half with chocolate icing. Put about 1 teaspoon of the filling on the remainder and top with the iced biscuit.

FILLING: Mix together egg, cornflour, milk and sugar. Cook over low heat, stirring constantly, until mixture boils and thickens. When cooled, fold in whipped cream or evaporated milk, vanilla, black coffee and brandy. Chill half an hour before using.

ICING: Dissolve cocoa and butter in the hot water, gradually beat in the icing sugar. Continue beating until icing is of spreading consistency. Beat in vanilla and cream of tartar.

Gerbeaud Slices

¼ oz. yeast
1 tablespoon sugar
¼ cup (2 oz.) milk
13 oz. plain flour
9 oz. butter
1 teaspoon castor sugar
1 whole egg
1 egg-yolk
½ teaspoon bicarbonate of soda
10 oz. walnuts
10 oz. castor sugar
3 oz. apricot conserve

Grind walnuts finely and combine castor sugar. Cream yeast with sugar, add milk and allow to stand for 1 hour. Rub between fingers flour, butter. Add castor sugar, whole egg, egg-yolk, the yeast mixture and bicarbonate of soda, and knead. Divide into 3 balls. Roll out each ball thinly and put one layer of pastry into a greased 9-in. or 8-in. square cake pan. Spread the top of the pastry with half apricot conserve and cover with half of walnut filling. Place second piece of pastry on top and spread with remainder of apricot conserve and cover with remainder of walnut filling. Place third layer of pastry on top. Bake at 350° for 30-35 minutes until golden brown. When cool, cut into fingers and ice every second one with a thin chocolate icing. This provides a nice contrast.

Walnut Cookies

(Makes 18)
1½ cups plain flour
½ teaspoon baking powder
¾ cup sugar
4 oz. butter
2 eggs
1 teaspoon golden syrup
½ teaspoon vanilla
½ teaspoon almond essence
½ cup walnuts, chopped finely
walnut halves for decoration

Sift flour, baking powder and sugar together. Cut in butter with knives or pastry blender until mixture resembles crumbs. Beat 1 egg slightly and stir into flour with golden syrup, vanilla, almond essence and walnuts. Shape into small balls and put 2 in. apart on ungreased baking trays. Mix remaining egg with 1 dessertspoon water and brush tops of cookies. Press walnut half into each one. Bake in moderately hot oven 10 to 12 minutes or until golden.

Brandy Crean

Croissants avec Pignons (Cinnamon Nut Crescents)

½ cup butter
½ cup white sugar
½ cup firmly-packed brown sugar
1 unbeaten egg
¼ cup pure fresh cream
1 teaspoon vanilla
2¼ cups self-raising flour
½ teaspoon salt
2 teaspoons cinnamon
1 cup finely-chopped unsalted peanuts

Cream well, butter, sugars; add unbeaten egg, cream and vanilla. Beat well. Blend in flour, salt and cinnamon gradually, mixing thoroughly. Roll dough by teaspoonsful on waxed paper with hands into cylinders about 2 in. long by ½ in. diameter. Roll in one cup unsalted peanuts. Place on ungreased baking sheets. Curve ends to form crescent shapes. Bake in moderate oven 350° 8-10 minutes. Makes approximately 6 dozen. These are crisp butter cookies with an intriguing cinnamon and brown sugar flavour and a crunchy coating of chopped unsalted peanuts—an authentic French specialty. In France they are served in an array of sweets at the Reveillon . . . that's the traditional midnight supper Frenchmen look forward to on Christmas Eve.

Chocolate Sesame Biscuits

4 oz. butter
2 oz. sugar
1 egg, beaten
½ cup dates, finely chopped
½ cup almonds, finely chopped
2 tablespoons sesame seeds
1 teaspoon sugar (extra)
1 cup (4 oz.) self-raising flour
½ cup cornflour
1 tablespoon cocoa
pinch salt

SESAME MIXTURE
1 tablespoon sugar
½ cup sesame seeds

Cream butter and sugar. Add egg beating well all the time. Combine dates, almonds, sesame seeds to which 1 teaspoon sugar has been added. Stir into creamed mixture. Sift together flour, cornflour, cocoa and salt. Fold into mixture. Mould mixture by teaspoonsful into small balls, then roll in the sesame seed mixture. Place on greased tray and flatten with the base of a glass. Bake in an oven 375°-400° for about 20 minutes.

Lemon Coconut Fingers

4 oz. butter
½ cup brown sugar
1 cup plain flour
pinch salt
chopped toasted almonds to decorate

FILLING
2 eggs
1 teaspoon vanilla
1 cup brown sugar
½ cup plain flour
1 teaspoon baking powder
pinch salt
1 cup shredded coconut
¾ cup finely chopped toasted blanched almonds

FROSTING
2 cups sifted icing sugar
¼ cup cream
grated rind 1 lemon
1 dessertspoon lemon juice

Cream butter and brown sugar until light and fluffy. Add sifted flour and salt and blend well. Press into buttered slab tin approximately 9-in. square. Bake in moderate oven 10 minutes. Cool in tin. Spread filling evenly over cooled base and bake further 20 minutes. Cool in tin and spread icing over. Sprinkle with almonds and cut into squares when cold.

FILLING: Beat eggs with vanilla and brown sugar until frothy. Sift flour, baking powder and salt twice. Fold into egg mixture. Add coconut and almonds, mix well.

FROSTING: Blend together icing sugar, cream, lemon rind and juice. Heat and stir over simmering water until shiny and smooth. Cool slightly.

Croissants avec Pignons (Cinnamon Nut Crescents)

Cream Cheese Spritz

(Makes 6 dozen)
2 cups plain flour
1 teaspoon baking powder
6 oz. butter
4 oz. cream cheese
1 cup sugar
1 egg
1 teaspoon grated lemon rind
1 dessertspoon milk
1 cup quick cooking oats
1 egg-white
1 tablespoon sugar
coloured sugar, optional

Sift together flour and baking powder. Mix butter and cream cheese together until smooth. Add to flour mixture with sugar, egg, lemon rind, milk and oats. Blend thoroughly. Chill 30 minutes. Force through cookie press on to ungreased baking tray. Beat egg-white until stiff but not dry. Gradually beat in 1 tablespoon sugar. Brush on cookies and decorate with coloured sugar. Bake in moderately hot oven 8 to 10 minutes.

Rum Jungle Jiffies

4 oz. butter
1 cup brown sugar
1 egg
1 cup dates
2 tablespoons hot water
2 tablespoons rum
1 tablespoon coffee essence
½ cup salted peanuts
½ cup coconut
2 cups self-raising flour
1 teaspoon each nutmeg and cinnamon

Cream butter and sugar, add egg and beat well. Mix together rum, coffee and hot water and pour over dates. Allow to stand 10 minutes; add to other ingredients. Add coconut and peanuts. Fold in sifted flour and spices. Press into greased lamington tin and bake 20 minutes in a moderately slow oven. When cold, ice with coffee icing flavoured with rum; sprinkle with peanuts. Cut into squares.

French Brittles

4 oz. butter
¼ cup castor sugar
grated rind of 1 lemon
grated rind of 1 orange
1 egg, separated
½ teaspoon vanilla
1 cup self-raising flour
1 tablespoon lemon juice
1 cup blanched almonds, finely chopped
glacé cherries to decorate

Cream butter and sugar, add orange and lemon rind, beaten egg-yolk and vanilla. Beat well. Add sifted flour, lemon juice and stir until well mixed and smooth. Cover and chill until firm. Form into small balls with floured hands. Dip each ball in beaten egg-white and then roll in chopped almonds. Put on well buttered baking tray and top each with half a cherry. Bake 15 to 20 minutes in moderate oven.

Chocolate Drop Cookies

(Makes 3 dozen)
1½ cups plain flour
¼ teaspoon salt
1 teaspoon baking powder
2 oz. chocolate
4 oz. butter, melted
1 cup brown sugar,
1 egg
½ cup milk
1 teaspoon vanilla
18 almonds, halved

Sift flour, salt and baking powder together. Melt chocolate and add to melted butter. Add brown sugar, egg, milk and vanilla then add sifted ingredients. Allow to stand 10 minutes. Drop from teaspoon on to buttered baking trays, place an almond half on each cookie and bake in moderate oven 12 to 15 minutes.

Butterscotch Brandy Bars

6 oz. butter
6 oz. sugar
12 oz. self-raising flour
2 eggs

FILLING
½ cup brandy
1 cup raisins
1 teaspoon instant coffee
1½ oz. butter
1½ oz. brown sugar
1 oz. plain flour
1 cup milk
2 oz. coconut
2 oz. chopped walnuts
2 tablespoons condensed milk

Cream together butter and sugar until light and fluffy, beat in eggs, gradually adding flour. Knead to a firm paste, adding a little more flour if it appears too sticky to roll out. Divide paste into two equal portions. Roll one piece out on to greaseproof or waxed paper, rectangular shape and just under ½ in. thick. Slide on to biscuit tray. Roll out second piece the same size, also on greased paper. Prepare fillings. Spread mixture evenly over paste on baking tray. Carefully take second piece of paste and place it over filling with the greaseproof uppermost. Peel paper off, press edges together with fork and prick at intervals. Bake at 350° for 40 minutes. Dust with icing sugar and cut into bars when cool.

FILLING: Simmer raisins and coffee in brandy over a high heat for 5 minutes. Set aside. Toast coconut and walnuts under griller until nicely browned. Melt butter and brown sugar in saucepan, blend in flour, add condensed milk. Gradually blend in milk. Cook until mixture thickens, add raisins and coconut and walnuts. Allow to cool slightly.

Macaroon Delights

4 oz. butter
1 oz. sugar
2 egg-yolks
8 oz. self-raising flour
pinch salt
1 tablespoon sherry

TOPPING
2 egg-whites
8 oz. ground almonds
4 oz. sugar
jam or jelly or whipped cream
a few glacé cherries to decorate

Cream butter till soft, add sugar, beat till dissolved. Beat in egg-yolks, stir in sifted flour and salt. Blend well, adding sherry and if necessary a small amount of water to make a stiff dough. Roll out on floured board $\frac{1}{8}$ in. thick. Cut into rounds with fluted cutter. Place biscuits on greased slide. Put topping mixture into piping bag with rose nozzle and pipe a ring round each biscuit. Bake in slow oven 300°-325° for 20 minutes or till golden brown. Cool on wire tray. Put $\frac{1}{2}$ teaspoon jam in centre of biscuit. For variation fill some with jelly or whipped cream and decorate with piece of cherry.

TOPPING: Whisk egg-whites until stiff, lightly fold in almonds, sugar.

Cheese and Ham Fingers

¾ cup plain flour
½ teaspoon cayenne
salt, pepper
2 oz. butter
3 oz. grated matured cheese
1 egg-yolk
good squeeze lemon juice

TOPPING
1 egg-white
1 cup finely minced ham

Sift flour, salt and pepper into a bowl, add cheese, rub in butter; mix to a dough with beaten egg-yolk and lemon juice. Roll out on floured board to a rectangle; cut into fingers. Bake in moderate oven 8 to 10 minutes. Beat egg-white until stiff, fold in ham and spread over the biscuits. Return to oven further 10 to 15 minutes or until golden brown. Cool on wire rack.

Walnut Ginger Butter Balls

8 oz. butter
½ cup icing sugar
1 teaspoon vanilla
2¼ cups plain flour
pinch salt
¾ cup chopped walnuts
4 oz. finely chopped preserved ginger
extra ¼ cup icing sugar
pinch ground ginger

Cream butter until light and creamy. Add sifted icing sugar, beat well, add vanilla. Stir in sifted flour and salt. Add walnuts. Take $\frac{1}{2}$ teaspoon of chopped ginger and mould a little mixture around it (about the size of a walnut). Bake on ungreased baking tray and in moderate oven about 15 minutes. Remove from tray, roll in sifted icing sugar and ground ginger, cool on rack. When cold roll again in sugar/ginger mixture.

Almond Sticks

8 oz. butter
½ cup sugar
1 egg
1 teaspoon almond essence
3 cups plain flour
pinch salt
beaten egg
½ cup finely chopped almonds
extra sugar

Cream butter and sugar. Add egg and almond essence, mix well. Stir in sifted flour and salt, knead until smooth. Chill 30 minutes, shape dough into long rolls about $\frac{1}{2}$ in. thick. Cut into $2\frac{1}{2}$-in. lengths, roll in beaten egg, then in almonds and sprinkle with sugar. Bake on buttered baking trays in moderate oven about 8 minutes until golden.

Macaroon Delights

Banana Lemon Bars

4 oz. butter
1 cup castor sugar
½ teaspoon lemon essence
2 eggs
1¾ cups plain flour
2 teaspoons baking powder
¼ teaspoon salt
1 dessertspoon instant coffee powder
1 cup mashed bananas
¼ cup finely chopped almonds or walnuts
¼ cup coconut
extra ¼ cup finely chopped toasted almonds to decorate

LEMON ICING
1½ cups sifted icing sugar
1½ oz. butter, melted
grated rind and juice of ½ lemon

Cream butter and sugar until light and fluffy. Add lemon essence and eggs and blend well. Sift flour, baking powder, salt and coffee twice. Add flour mixture alternately with the mashed banana and almonds. Spread into buttered and papered slab tin, 9-in. square. Bake in moderate oven about 30 minutes. Cool in tin. Frost cake with lemon icing and sprinkle with chopped toasted almonds blended with coconut. When set, cut into bars.

LEMON ICING: Blend together in a bowl the icing sugar, butter, lemon rind and juice to a spreading consistency.

Delicate French Fingers

2½ cups plain flour
8 oz. butter
1 tablespoon vinegar
⅓ cup water
⅔ cup sugar

FRENCH FILLING
6 oz. butter
3 oz. sifted pure icing sugar
1 egg-yolk
1 teaspoon vanilla

Sift flour into mixing bowl. Cut in butter until mixture resembles coarse breadcrumbs. Mix vinegar and water and sprinkle on dry mixture 1 tablespoon at a time, gently tossing with a fork. Continue to add water mixture to dry mixture until dough is just moist enough to hold together. Divide dough into 2 balls and chill 20 minutes. Remove 1 ball and roll out ⅛ in. thick, cut into oblong shapes 2 in. x 1 in. Put sugar on wax paper and press biscuit shapes on lightly to make sugar cling. Transfer sugar-side up to ungreased baking trays and bake in very hot oven 8 to 10 minutes or until top begins to caramelize. Roll out remaining dough the same way. When cool sandwich fingers with filling.

FRENCH FILLING: Cream butter until light, add icing sugar then egg-yolk and vanilla. Beat until smooth and creamy.

Honey Walnut Cluster

FILLING
½ cup finely chopped dates
2 tablespoons water
1 teaspoon lemon juice
¼ teaspoon cinnamon
1 tablespoon honey
¼ cup chopped walnuts

BISCUIT MIXTURE
4 oz. butter
¼ cup firmly packed brown sugar
¼ cup sifted icing sugar
1 egg
½ teaspoon vanilla essence
1 cup (4 oz.) self-raising flour
½ cup (2 oz.) plain flour
½ cup cornflour
pinch salt

FILLING: Mix dates, water, lemon juice and cinnamon together, place in a small saucepan over gentle heat. Simmer for five minutes until dates are soft. Remove from heat, stir in honey and walnuts, set aside to cool.

BISCUIT MIXTURE: Cream together butter and sugars until fluffy. Add beaten egg and vanilla essence, beat well. Sift together flours and salt, then work into the creamed mixture, making a rather firm dough. Shape into 21 balls, reserving enough dough for stem and two leaf shapes. Make a deep indentation in each ball with thumb and fill with portion of cooled filling mixture and mould over to cover filling. Line a large baking sheet with foil. Arrange prepared biscuits on foil to resemble V-shaped cluster, each biscuit just touching. Roll out reserved dough to ¼ in. thickness. Cut into two leaf shapes with serrated biscuit cutter. Mark veins in deeply with back of knife blade. Arrange on baking sheet with biscuit cluster, shape short stem from any remaining dough pieces, arrange in place. Bake in hot oven (400°G, 425°E) 20 minutes, until golden and crisp. Serve while warm and fragrant, with butter curls or just plain.

Praline Crunch Nuggets

½ cup brown sugar
1 tablespoon butter
½ cup blanched, split almonds (walnuts or peanuts can be used)
1 cup self-raising flour
½ cup plain flour
¼ teaspoon salt
4 oz. butter
⅓ cup brown sugar
1 small egg
1 teaspoon vanilla

ICING MIXTURE
3 tablespoons icing sugar
1 tablespoon cocoa
1 teaspoon cinnamon

Put first measure of sugar into a heavy bottomed saucepan over low heat, stirring till golden brown. Add butter, then nuts, stir around till mixture holds together, take up, pour on to greased wax paper, let cool. Chop small when cold. Sift flours and salt together. Cream butter and sugar well together, add beaten egg and vanilla. Mix well. Blend in sifted dry ingredients. Add the chopped praline crunch. Lift approximately a dessertspoonful, at a time, round into a ball, place on ungreased baking tray, cook in slow oven 25 to 30 minutes. While hot, roll in icing mixture.

ICING MIXTURE: Sift together icing sugar, cocoa, cinnamon. Place on wax paper. In this roll the hot nuggets.

Cashew-topped Ginger Bars

4 oz. butter
2 oz. castor sugar
4 oz. self-raising flour
1 level teaspoon ground ginger
pinch salt

TOPPING

4 level tablespoons icing sugar
2 level tablespoons butter
1 level teaspoon ground ginger
3 level teaspoons golden syrup
4 oz. chopped toasted cashew nuts

Cream butter and sugar. Add sifted dry ingredients and mix thoroughly until well absorbed. Press into greased slab tin 7 in. x 11 in. and bake in moderate oven (375°F.) until slightly brown, 15-20 minutes. Pour topping over biscuit layer while both are still warm and sprinkle with chopped cashew nuts. Cut into bars when cool.

TOPPING: Place all ingredients (except nuts) in saucepan. Stir over gentle heat until butter is melted and ingredients well mixed.

Australian Curry Biscuits

2 cups self-raising flour
½ teaspoon salt
1 teaspoon mustard
pinch cayenne
1½ teaspoons curry powder
⅔ cup butter
1 cup grated sharp cheddar cheese
1 egg
2 tablespoons milk

Combine sifted flour with salt, mustard, curry powder and cayenne. Work in butter with fingertips, stir in cheese, beaten egg and milk. Work lightly with fingertips until dough holds together. Turn on to floured board, roll to $\frac{1}{16}$ in. thickness. Cut out with floured 2-in. cutter (or cut into cheese-straw or other shapes). Bake in hot oven 10 minutes. Biscuits can be brushed with egg glazing before baking and sprinkled with sesame seeds, poppy seeds, grated cheese or crushed rock salt.
(See frontispiece illustration)

Holiday Spritz

1 cup soft butter
⅔ cup sugar
3 egg-yolks
1 teaspoon rum flavouring
2½ cups plain flour

BUTTER RUM GLAZE

¼ cup butter
1 cup sifted icing sugar
1 teaspoon rum flavouring
1 or 2 tablespoons hot water

Heat oven to 400°. Mix butter, sugar, egg-yolks and flavouring thoroughly. Work in sifted flour. Roll out thinly and cut into desired shapes, or force dough through a biscuit press. Place biscuits on ungreased baking sheet and bake 7-10 minutes until set, but not brown. This quantity makes 6 dozen biscuits. Glaze cooled biscuits with Butter Rum Glaze.

BUTTER RUM GLAZE: Melt butter in saucepan. Blend in icing sugar and rum flavouring. Stir in 1 to 2 tablespoons hot water until glaze spreads smoothly. Tint glaze to match biscuits.

Light-as-air Crisps

8 oz. butter
3 oz. castor sugar
2 tablespoons hot water
2 teaspoons vanilla essence
8 oz. plain flour
2 oz. chopped walnuts

Cream butter and castor sugar until fluffy. Add hot water, vanilla essence and plain flour. Stir well then add walnuts. The mixture will be soft so wrap in aluminium foil and leave in the refrigerator for 2-3 hours till firm. When ready to bake set oven at 325°F. Roll small pieces of the dough into 4-in. lengths with the palms of the hands on a slightly floured board. Then shape pieces into crescents. Put on ungreased baking slides, bake for 15 minutes, until firm but pale. Leave to cool for 5 minutes, then roll in icing sugar.

Cashew-topped Ginger Bars

Candy and Spice Honey Chews

4 oz. butter
2 oz. sugar
4 oz. honey
1 egg
a few drops lemon essence
8 oz. self-raising flour
2 teaspoons cocoa
1 teaspoon cinnamon
½ teaspoon nutmeg
¼ teaspoon mace
pinch salt
½ cup chopped walnuts
¼ cup walnut pieces for decorating

HONEY TOFFEE
2 oz. butter
2 oz. sugar
3 oz. honey
1 tablespoon water
3 oz. desiccated coconut

Preheat oven to 350°. Butter oven slides. Cream butter, sugar and honey. Add well-beaten egg, cream well. Add essence. Sift dry ingredients twice, then blend into the creamed mixture and add chopped walnuts. Place small spoonsful on tray. With the back of teaspoon handle hollow out centres. Place a small ball of Honey Toffee (size of marble) in each. Top each one with a piece of walnut. Bake for 10 minutes. Remove from slide, cool on rack. Yields approximately 4½ dozen.

HONEY TOFFEE: Place in a saucepan the butter, sugar, honey and water and bring to boil, boil for 8-10 minutes. Remove from heat and stir in coconut. Cool.

Poppy Seed Trifles

1½ cups plain flour
½ teaspoon salt
4 oz. butter
4 oz. packet cream cheese
3 tablespoons sugar
¼ teaspoon lemon essence
1 dessertspoon poppy seeds

Sift flour and salt. Cream butter and add cream cheese, blend well. Add 2 tablespoons sugar and beat until light, then add lemon essence. Stir in flour mixture lightly, chill. Shape into small balls about ½ in. in diameter, put on lightly buttered baking trays. Press each one twice with a fork to make a criss-cross design on top. Sprinkle with poppy seeds and remaining sugar. Bake in moderate oven 10 to 12 minutes.

Hazelnut Snaps

(Makes 3 dozen)
4 oz. butter
⅓ cup castor sugar
3 oz. ground hazelnuts
½ teaspoon vanilla
1½ cups plain flour
pinch salt

Cream butter and sugar until light and fluffy. Blend in ground hazelnuts and vanilla. Add sifted flour and salt and mix thoroughly to form a dough. Form into rolls 1 in. in diameter and chill 1 to 2 hours. Cut into thin slices and place on buttered baking trays. Bake in moderate oven 12 to 15 minutes.

Fudge Fingers

4 oz. butter
1 cup self-raising flour
¾ cup sugar
½ cup cherries, finely chopped
½ cup finely chopped walnuts
1 tablespoon coconut
1 dessertspoon cocoa
pinch salt
1 egg, beaten
icing sugar

Rub butter into sifted flour. Add sugar, cherries, walnuts, coconut, cocoa and salt. Stir in egg, mix well together into a ball. Press out with hand to fit a buttered tin (10 in. x 7 in.). Bake in moderate oven 20 minutes. Cut into strips while hot and leave in tin until cold. Dust with icing sugar.

Candy and Spice Honey Che

Gingerunes

2 cups sifted plain flour
1 teaspoon bicarbonate of soda
¼ teaspoon salt
1 teaspoon ginger
¼ teaspoon cloves, powdered
½ teaspoon cinnamon
⅔ cup brown sugar
4 oz. butter
1 unbeaten egg
¼ cup molasses or treacle
1 cup coconut
48 pitted soft prunes
water
granulated sugar

Sift together flour, soda, salt and spices. Cream butter and sugar, add egg and molasses, beat well. Add dry ingredients, mix well, add coconut. If possible chill for about ½ hour. Then flatten one teaspoon of dough for each biscuit. Place prune in centre, shaping dough around it. Dip top in water then in sugar. Place sugar side up on ungreased tray. Bake 12-15 minutes, moderate oven 375°. Makes approximately 4 dozen. If liked, ice ¼ with white icing, ¼ with pink, and leave half un-iced.

Brown Rim Cookies

1 cup plain flour
½ cup cornflour
1½ teaspoons cream of tartar
¾ cup butter
1 cup castor sugar
½ teaspoon vanilla
1 large egg
½ cup finely slivered blanched almonds

Sift together plain flour, cornflour and cream of tartar. Cream butter, sugar and vanilla, beat in the egg thoroughly, mix in the sifted ingredients until blended. Drop slightly heaped teaspoonsful of the dough, at least 2 in. apart, on a cookie sheet. Place one piece of slivered blanched almonds in the centre of each cookie. Bake in a hot (400°) oven for 6 to 8 minutes or until cookies have wide brown rims and centres are still white. Remove carefully with a wide spatula to a wire rack to cool. Store these fragile crisp cookies in a tightly covered metal container. Makes about 6 dozen.